SPIRITUAL RESUME

SPIRITUAL RESUME

Wounded Warrior Newly Nourished
Making Meaningful Movements

LAQUISHA MARTIN-HILLIAN

MILL CITY PRESS

Mill City Press, Inc.
2301 Lucien Way #415
Maitland, FL 32751
407.339.4217
www.millcitypress.net

Paperback ISBN-13: 978-1-66283-429-5
Ebook ISBN-13: 978-1-66283-430-1

This is giving honor and all the glory to one Man. The Man who sits high and looks low. The Man who has always provided me with the reassurance I need and needed to get through life.

Lord, My Father, thank You once again for directing my path.

TABLE OF CONTENTS

Chapter One

MY FIRST LOVE

"I am the vine: you are the branches. If you remain in me and I in you, you will bear much fruit, for apart from me you can do nothing" John 15:5

Throughout this book, I am called "LaQuisha, Quisha, Qrish, and Keisha. I'm not sure why, but I answered to them all. My first love did not call my name. I met my first love in third grade. It was love at first sight, but I didn't know it would be the start of something so joyful and so painful. It was an instant attraction. My first love allowed me to be free. Free from pain, disappointments, and fear. My first love spoke every time I needed it to. Swish! It was a beautiful sound. I loved the sound it made. Whether we were in front of others or alone. I knew how I felt and how my first love made me feel. I felt like I was the only one in the room. My first love allowed me to pick it up any time, day or night. Holding it under my arms or in my hands brought me a sense of peace. Many touched and held it, but I knew it was committed to me as I was committed to it. Oh, how my first love came through for me many times. It failed me more times than I could count, but that's love. Still, we found our way back to each other. My sweat never stopped it from going through the net. No matter the goal's position on an old tree, on a piece of plywood, or in a gymnasium, my first love gave me points time after time. I was myself around my first love. When I was upset, or hurt, I pounded my first love into the pavement, dirt, or gymnasium floor. My first love never felt abused or misused. As a matter of fact, that was the job of my first love. There were times my first love rolled or bounced away. I could always go and pick it up again. When I was joyful and filled with peace, I loved on my first love, and gently bounced it around my legs from left hand to right hand. The more I became one with my first love, the more confident I became in the presence of others. My first love was how others saw me in a different light. Oh, my first love and I "showed out" most nights. The people cheered us on as I took my first love and shot it in the net repeatedly. My first love brought me closer to God. Being with my first love, I learned the Lord's Prayer

"Our Father in heaven,
hallowed be your name,
your kingdom come,
your will be done,
on earth as it is in heaven.
Give us today our daily bread.

And forgive us our debts,
as we also have forgiven our debtors.
And lead us not into temptation,
but deliver us from the evil one"
Matthew 6:9-13

Lord, trust was something I've learned to do with You by experience. Lord, I've had my fair share of doubt if You really were there for me. It took time to surrender to You. I recall the moments I did. Junior year in high school: the torn ACL of my right knee. Lord, basketball was all I thought I had. It was the gift You gave to me. Basketball was the core of my family. All the women in my family played and I understood why. It gave me a joy, regardless of what went on. When I stepped on that court, nothing else mattered. So, when I went out on the court I didn't talk to people, really, I just played ball. Then the day I went down and didn't come back up changed my body, my emotions, my spirit, and started my trust in You.

At practice Mr. Harris (basketball coach) said, "QRISH (coach never called me LaQuisha or Quisha), run this with them." It was the Figure Eight, and I had just gone down, but he wanted me to be co-captain, so I went again. I didn't want to, but I ran down, went up for a shot, came down, and I heard a loud pop. Down I went, screaming in pain. It seemed like my knee was on fire and the flames came up my leg throughout my body. Others heard the pop too.

As I grabbed my knee I heard, "Oh Lawd, Qrish," from Coach Harris. I heard, "There goes y'all season," from a previous player.

I saw Coach Bobby, and he asked, "Where are you hurting?" I told him as I cried and held on to my leg. He shook his head and said, "Harris, this doesn't look good at all."

For me, I had no idea what was in store. My friends and teammates were there but the pain overwhelmed me. All I thought about was, "Will I get up and play again?"

Once I arrived from the hospital and went home, familiar faces were right there: my cousins, my grandmother, my mother, and my sisters. I cried when they all left my room. The doctors weren't sure what was wrong, so I had to go see a specialist. Just when things were going well, God, what did I do?

> *"And whatever you do, in word or deed do everything in the name of the Lord Jesus, giving thanks to God the Father through him." Colossians 3:17*

I went to the doctor, and he said he wasn't sure if I could play for the season. That was a big season for me. I felt I had a chance to make all conference. I could not believe how I could work so hard, and do the one thing I enjoyed doing, but have it taken away from me. I spoke to Mr. O (trainer for the school). I begged him to speak with the doctor because he was the one who recommended him.

"Please help, Mr. O, this is my year." As I cried and begged, all he did was drop his head. He already knew what I didn't know, which was I would need surgery sooner than later. He told me to be patient and wait to see what the knee would do. I left on those hard, stiff substitute legs most call crutches. My heart was in pieces, my dreams, plans no more. "Lord, what will I do if I can't play ball?"

"These people honor me with their lips but their hearts are far from me..." Matthew 15:8

I went to practice every day and watched on the sidelines as someone else played a position I had so rightfully earned and worked hard for. There was a maintenance man who watched us practice every day. He was a kind individual, but I never knew his name. One day he came up to me and asked, "Do you want to get back out there?"

My look was like, "Man, the doctor said I'm done for the season." Still, I responded, "Yes, sir."

He then asked, "Do you believe you can get back out there and play ball?"

I wanted to scream, "Please leave me alone," but I said, "I don't know."

He said, "If you believe in God, you can get back on that court."

I just looked at him. He did not know my past, the anger and despair I had in my heart. The loved ones taken too soon. He did not know my heart's pain. Or did he?

He looked at me and said, "I see your pain, but if you believe in God and do what I say, you can be back on that basketball court." He then gave me a bottle with oil in it. He said, "Place this oil on your knee and pray each time." He never said how many times or what to pray, he just said, "Put it on your knee and pray."

As he walked away, I looked at the bottle of oil. I knew what my grandpa said about the oil and how it could heal, but what puzzled me was, "Why my family didn't think about it?" I knew I had nothing to lose. So, I went into the locker room, placed the oil on my leg, and prayed. Did I know this would work? Nope. I knew I wanted to get out there and play basketball. What I realized was the more I prayed, the less I worried about not playing.

> *"Do not be anxious about anything, but in everything by prayer and supplication with thanksgiving let your request be made known to God. And the peace of God, which surpasses all understanding, will guard your hearts and your minds in Christ Jesus..."*
> *Philippians 4:6-7*

Now, I see this happened because I placed my focus on God. The problem remained the same, but God became bigger than the problem. A junior in high school tried to place God before her situation. Do you believe that? Well, I got back on that court, but it was hard to trust my knee. That was immaturity. I thought once I returned, I would be the same physically. The question was, "Was it physically, mentally, or spiritually that I changed?"

The first game of my return, I missed so many free throws. I shot the last free throw and missed again. My head dropped so hard from the defeat in my mind. "I will never be the same." The truth was, I wasn't the same. I prayed to return to the game, but I didn't pray for the courage I needed to return.

Mr. Harris said as we walked side-by-side to the locker room, "Qrish, come on, girl, you can do it. Trust the knee. I know it's hard, but you can't give up and you can't be scared to bend that knee."

I heard him but I was scared: What if it popped again? What if I hurt the knee again? what if I fell?

Well, we lost that game, and all I knew was I didn't like feeling defeated or afraid to bend my knee. The next day in practice, I isolated from everyone. I went to a separate basket. I practiced my free throws. My best friend/sister Le'Tasha came over to rebound the ball.

She said, "You can do it, Quisha."

Tears rolled from my eyes. If only she knew I was scared, hurt. This one thing that brought me joy and took me from reality caused me tremendous fear. She felt my pain, and she had a sad look upon her face as well. God placed someone special in my life, Le'Tasha. Whenever you saw her, I was there; whenever you saw me, she was there. If you didn't, we were close by and on the way. She was the support I needed. She helped me through this storm. I am not sure about the games in between, but I recalled the game when I conquered my fear.

> *"No, in all these things we are more than conquerors through him who loved us."*
> *Romans 8:37*

The team we played when I bombed all the free throws, we had to play again, but this time on our court. They came for me, but what they didn't know I wasn't scared or weak anymore. My first love and I played ball that night. This time, I gave them what I had: *confidence*. You see, in between those games, I continued to pray and placed oil on my knee. What I did differently was to ask God for help. I needed courage; I wanted that fear to go away. I needed to get back what I lost: *joy*. Free throw after free throw, I talked to myself, but also I spoke to God. The more I prayed, the smaller the fear. I could bend my knee, which was always the case. The fear diminished and God became bigger.

> *"Behold I am doing a new thing; now it springs forth, do you not perceive it? I will make a way in the wilderness and rivers in the desert." Isaiah 43:19* ESV

After the game, Mr. Harris said, "Qrish, I told you, you got your niche back, you just had to trust the knee." In my mind, I had to "*Trust God.*"

As the games took place, I gave my all, but it wasn't enough. I didn't receive all conference, which was hurtful to me. The janitor later spoke with me. He said, "You feel different, don't you?"

"Yes sir, I think I do."

He said, "Life will bring you many challenges. Despite how you feel or what it is, *pray.*"

You know what I didn't know then? Something would soon come to rock my world and I would need God to see me through it. God had a way and sent people or things to give a message. That janitor was my message from God, I was just too young to truly hear Him because a storm came and shook my family tremendously.

> *"I am the vine: you are the branches. If you remain in me and I in you, you will bear much fruit, for apart from me you can do nothing" John 15:5*

Chapter Two

DEATH KNOCKS... 1, 2, 3, 4

"Do not let your hearts be troubled. You believe in God; believe also in me. My Father's house has many rooms; if that were not so would I have told you that I am going there to prepare a place for you? And if I go and prepare a place for you, I will come back and take you to be with me that you also may be where I am. You know the way to the place where I am going." John 14:1-4

Those who knew me, knew I was afraid of death. Death took my loved ones. Death brought pain to my heart that lingered for what seemed like forever. Death, why did you come? Death, why take and not give? Death, why not give warning so I could say my goodbyes? Death, you came time and time again, and I'm tired of you. Tired, I say! Death, when will you stop? Why won't you stop? Death, I'm sick to my stomach because you lingered around the corner and then **boom**, my world exploded. Death, one day, I will find a way to not give you so much energy. Well, Death, listen to what you did to me. Death, once each year throughout high school, you took away the most important men in my life. ***Death, I don't like you!*** You listen, listen to my cry: pain, you caused, **Death**!

Poboy (my uncle)

> *"but we are of good courage and prefer rather
> to be absent from the body and to be at home
> with the Lord." 2 Corinthians 5:8*

It was a normal day. I was a freshman in high school. My mother picked me up from a softball game. I jumped in the car, and she said, "Your uncle is home."

Now let me clue you in on my Uncle Poboy. He went to the hospital a lot for different reasons but returned. It was just the process. However, this time, he went to the hospital but didn't seem like himself. My uncle's legs were amputated many years ago. He had an ulcer on his elbow because he spent most of the day pressed on it as he held himself up with the hospital bed sling attached to the bed. And he Poboy talked alot.

We arrived home, I jumped out the car and ran down the hallway to his room. I was so fast, my grandma did not have the chance to say, "Don't run in this house." I raced to his room, where I watched how he struggled to breathe. His stomach went so far in, his stomach and chest were the same. Nothing was on, no TV or music. Just him breathing hard and heavy, as he leaned forward on his left arm, which was around the armrest sling of his bed.

Well, I said, "How are you, and why are you breathing like that?"

He said, "None of your business and go get me some cold water."

My uncle had a **huge** drinking cup and I filled it up with ice and water. He drank it fast, and he told me to get more. He sent me back to get the third cup. As I went into the kitchen, I heard "Don't you take anymore ice water back there, you hear me?" It was my grandma, and as I looked up, she was sewing the entire time. So, I went to his room told him what Grandma said and he said, "Okay." What seemed strange was he told me to leave the room. It wasn't in those exact words, but he told me to leave.

I ironically said, "No, I'm fine, I can stay."

As stated before, my Uncle Poboy was an amputee. He would call all day, all night for something, and we as his nieces and nephews had to help. So, we would say, "You take it, no you take it, I took it the last time." We were kids, we didn't know any better. All we knew, he stopped us from whatever we were doing. Which was trouble, LOL. So, I told him I would stay, but he insisted I leave, which struck me as very odd. I went, but slowly.

I got ready for bed. But before I got into bed, my grandma said, "Keisha, go back there and tell Poboy I will bring his pills in a minute."

I walked down the hallway. His room was at the end of the hallway, and it was dark. I couldn't see anything, and it frightened me. I stopped in the middle of the hallway and yelled, "Poboy, Grandma said she will be back there to give you your pills in a few minutes." All I heard was a very weak, "Okay," and I slowly bagged up and went to my room.

It wasn't long before I heard my grandma call, "**Biiillllll,** hurry, hurry."

I jumped out of bed and ran down the hallway like everyone else. I ran to his room, and everyone called his name, but he didn't respond. So, I turned and my mother was in the doorway. I looked at her, but she didn't understand my look. She didn't know my thoughts, which was, "He was dead!" I could not speak. I didn't say give him mouth to mouth. It was as if I did not have the ability to speak.

In seconds the paramedic came through the door. He was a short chubby white guy who knew us all so well because of the many times we had to call 911. As soon as he saw my uncle, he immediately cut his white t-shirt up the middle and said, "**Get out now!**" It did not register in my head what he said. All I knew was Grandma would whip his butt for cutting up my uncle's white t-shirt. Yes, he had plenty of shirts, but still, he cut up my uncle's shirt.

As my thoughts raced through my mind, everything happened so fast. Someone swept me up from his room and rushed me up the hallway. We heard my uncle's heart being shocked repeatedly. Grandpa said, "There it goes again," each time they shocked his heart. Then my grandma said,

"Shut up, just shut up!" They both sat in their recliners in the living room.

My grandma continued to sew her clothes from earlier and my grandpa sat with his head downward. My Aunt Mary and I were in the kitchen, which was not as big as a match box, but as she held me, the paramedic brought my uncle up the hallway in his arms. Usually, he fussed as they carried him up the hallway, but not this time. This time he had a tube in his mouth, but his lifeless body could not accept the fluids. The more my aunt and I told him to fight, the more it seemed he was defeated. His body was lifeless before our eyes.

In my mind, I asked myself questions. "What happened? How did it happen? Why would they send him home if he wasn't okay"? As we ran to the porch, my cousin Nate was there along with many others. My cousin Nate was a part of the *Big 5* (Poboy, Nate, Jamesbrown, Grandpa, and me). He had me to cook for him and fix his plate, and kept me motivated about basketball. Well, Nate reassured me he would go check on Poboy and call me to let me know. That's what he said, but you know it didn't happen. While the ambulance took my uncle, my mother, Aunt Kay, and others followed behind the ambulance. I can't recall where all the other kids were, my little cousins and sisters (Tasha, James, Jerry, Kat, and my sisters, Nikki and Chris). As I waited with Grandma, Grandpa, Aunt Bill, and Uncle Jake, I forgot about what happened. I was on the sofa with butter pecan ice cream and a chocolate cupcake stuck in the middle of it. Yes, I liked it like that. The phone rang and my Aunt Bill answered it and all she said was, "Okay, okay, okay, okay."

My grandma said, "Give me the phone," and then she said, "You tell me, you tell me now, I say. Okay, don't tell me, but I know I know."

I didn't figure it out, but a part of me knew, like my grandma, that he had died. Well, time went by, and I heard a car pull up, and like always I could hear my Uncle Poboy fussing in the back seat as loud as he could. The ironic thing was I heard nothing, just the doors closed and footsteps. My Aunt Kay entered the room with her big eyes red as fire, head lowered, and tears in her eyes.

My grandma said, "He's gone right, he's gone." As I looked at Grandma in shock, I glazed back at my aunt, whose tears flowed from her face.

She said slowly and hesitantly, "Yes he's gone, Ma."

Grandma continued, "I knew it, I knew it before he left."

My grandpa said nothing, just shook his head continuously. It took a moment for it to register in my head, but when it did, I dropped that ice cream and ran in the bathroom banged on the wall. I wanted to find something to take the pain away. He was here one minute and gone the next. I needed to hit something because the pain within me was so unbearable that I couldn't breathe. As my Uncle Jake consoled me, I ran out the door into the living room, down the steps, and up the hill. I ran without shoes and in my gown. I tried to reach him myself. I wanted to see for myself. I ran because I thought if he saw me run toward him, he would come toward me.

I couldn't make the pain go away. I couldn't stop the ache my heart felt. As I reached the curve, my cousin Jamesbrown came around the corner, as my grandma said, "Like a bat out of hell." I turned around and chased his Bronco. I had to let him know we needed to go to the hospital. I had to let him know Poboy was dead. I had to let him know we needed to help him. I reached the bottom of the hill and ran up the steps. I looked and didn't see him. I heard his cry from my uncle's room.

He said, "I didn't say goodbye, Grandma, I didn't say goodbye. I didn't come by today, I didn't come by today."

As we cried together, we laid on his bed and pleaded for him to return. We asked for help from the Man above. We asked Grandma to take it away, to bring him back.

I remember she said, "Get your cry out, go ahead and cry. This is what he wanted, to come home and die, so you go ahead and cry, but don't cry too long, it will make you sick."

I don't remember the moments after that, and I don't wish to do so. All I remember is the uncle who called us for every little thing, the uncle who laughed his butt off when we were punished, the uncle who defended us if we were right was gone.

Cousin Nate

*"Come to me, all you who are weary and bur-
dened, and I will give you rest. Take my yoke
upon you and learn from me, for I am gentle
and humble in heart, and you will find rest
for your souls. For my yoke is easy and my
burden is light." Matthew 11:28-30*

It took some time for me to get over my uncle's death. The house wasn't the same without him. It seemed quiet and lonely. People who would come visit my uncle stopped coming. One of those persons was Nate. My cousin Nate was much older than I was, but he treated me like I was so much older. He always wanted to know how many points I scored and to cook chicken skin whenever he came to our house.

"Chicken skin, Grandma throws that away." He said, "That's the good part."

Me, "No it really isn't, that's why she threw it away." Like my grandma didn't have enough in her kitchen, on the stove, or in the refrigerator, lol.

If I didn't take water to Poboy, I fried meat skin for Nate, fried six eggs for Jamesbrown, or ate Vienna wieners and saltine crackers with my grandpa. The thought of that food makes me sick now, LOL. I was in my sophomore year, and it was basketball season at that time.

I had a basketball game the night before and I was tired and sore the next morning. My grandmother came into my uncle's room. I slept on the floor because I couldn't find it in my heart at the time to sleep in his bed. "Keisha, get up now, I done told you, ain't going to tell you no mo."

As I slowly got up, I remember she said Nate died. When I finally got up, she came back in the room and said, "He died last night." Of course, I was half asleep, so I wasn't sure what she said, but I said, "Okay." My grandma of course was shocked because of my lack of emotion. It wasn't until I reached the bathroom when it hit me: "Nate is dead?" I repeated it because for some reason, I could not figure out who Nate was. I had a delay in my brain that would not process. I hadn't seen Nate in so long. He stopped coming by after my Uncle Poboy died and when he got that new girlfriend, I never saw him. I went to the bathroom, and it was then as I turned on the water, I realized what my grandma said: "Nate is dead." As I cried quietly in the bathroom, I couldn't believe it. My uncle last year, now my cousin. Did I do something wrong, have I said something that I shouldn't have?

It was the mirror I broke. I recalled I broke a mirror and Grandma said, "Seven years of bad luck." Did this mean I had five more deaths to go through? After I got ready, I got in my Uncle Rob's car because I missed the bus again, and believe it or not, he didn't fuss at me not one time. He worked third shift and hated to come home to see one of us needing a ride to school because we missed the bus.

Sometimes we did it just because we didn't want to ride that slow, musty bus. As he drove me to school, he said, in his deep concerned and hurtful voice, "It will be okay. Stop crying, your eyes are going to swell."

I dropped my head and didn't care about my eyes at all. Of course, that's all I remember of that day, but I recall the day of the funeral.

I had on a green dress of my mother's because I didn't own a dress. It just wasn't my thang. The dress was so fitting, and I felt like all eyes were on me, but of course they weren't. I went to the casket and looked at him, like "Who is this in this casket?" Were we at the wrong funeral, have I cried over someone else's cousin? But family called his name and yelled out for him, but what happened? I knew when someone died things changed, but I didn't know who he was. So, I slowly moved away from the casket. What I knew: **I was angry at God!**

> "Be merciful to me, Lord, for I am in distress; my eyes grow weak with sorrow, my soul and body with grief. My life is consumed by anguish and my years by groaning, my strength fails because of my affliction, and my bones grow weak." Psalm 31:9-10

> "The Lord is close to the brokenhearted and saves those who are crushed in spirit." Psalm 34:18

Just when I obtained a sense of normalcy, a tornado took my family in and just wouldn't let go. This next storm changed my family forever not even my first love could fix this one.

Cousin Jamesbrown

> *The Lord is close to the brokenhearted and saves those who are crushed in spirit".* *Psalm 34:18*

Jamesbrown fixed bikes up for us. He was in trouble a lot and needed company, so we all went along with it. When he got older, he moved out. I do recall when he took my phone out of my room. Okay true, I didn't use the phone much, but it was the principle of the matter. He didn't live there anymore, it wasn't his room anymore, and my Uncle Poboy wasn't there anymore, so I felt it was disrespectful. Well, one night he called and begged for me to get on the phone, and I refused. I held my silent treatment until I exploded. I didn't know it would be the last time I spoke with him. However, my mother said it wasn't, because I took a dinner plate to his apartment and saw the fish he had in his tank.

I wanted to believe this with all my heart, but I can't remember the order in which everything transpired. I went to his apartment and took the plate, but I'm still not sure if that was before or after the fight. As I wrote this, I realized my mother was right, because he said, "Do you forgive me now?" All these years, I thought he died and I was still mad at him, but before I left, we laughed. I didn't have a choice because he tickled me.

So, to my surprise, it was a Sunday, I was in church, and my leg was in a brace (that torn ACL). You think when you are in the house of the Lord you are protected; no harm, danger, or bad news can touch you. Not true, not true at all.

My mom went to the back of the church, and she yelled, "Keisha, let's go, Jamesbrown been shot!" I couldn't run because I had a brace on my knee, but I tried to move as fast as I could. The events are not clear, but I remember my mother drove to his apartment, blew the horn the entire way. I cried, she cried. I imagined him on the floor bleeding and calling out to Grandma. That was in my head, but reality was quite different.

We arrived. Everyone was there. The road and driveway were filled with people. I remember Jeannette was up against the tree with my Uncle Dan. I was placed in the car with Jamesbrown's mom. She cried so much, her cry sounded weak and exhausted. She continued to cry out for her baby, but he couldn't hear her. She begged God, as I tried to bargain with God with her. We tried, but God didn't hear us. Then the door opened, and a stretcher was pushed out. On it was a black bag. I wasn't sure what it was until, I heard, "Nooooo, my baby, oh God, nooooo, please, not my baby!" It was Jamesbrown in the black bag.

"Wait, Wait," I screamed as I jumped out the back seat of the car. "WAIT!" I needed to see for myself, but someone grabbed me and turned me away from him. "No, please, please, Jamesbrown, Jamesbrown, Jamesbrown! Please! Please!" I forgot my leg, I forgot I had the brace on my leg. I just needed to see him, but I couldn't. Anger and rage filled my heart.

Who would do something like that? Who could take his life and leave him? Why, Lord, why? *"No temptation has overtaken you that is not common to man. God is faithful, and he will not let you be tempted beyond your ability, but with the temptation he will also provide the way to escape, that you may be able to endure it". 1 Corinthians 10:13 ESV*

Eventually we went home to Grandma. My grandma came and said, "Keisha, baby you got to stop crying, you are going to make yourself sick."

I said, "Ma, why do they keep dying, why do they keep leaving me?"

Ma said, "Baby, we all must leave this world someday, it's not meant for us to stay."

"Grandma, please Grandma, please, I can't do this no more, please, Grandma, make it stop, please!"

I heard my cousins' and sisters' cries. As we hugged on each other, I thought, "Who will be next?"

Of course, death came when my guard was down. It seemed like once I began to get back to the normalcy I once knew, another storm came. This time I kept watch, but things went well for a long time. I got comfortable, I was happy, I moved into a place where I didn't feel pain. Until...

Grandpa: Bo Martin

"Humble yourselves, therefore, under God's mighty hand, that he may lift you up in due time. Cast all your anxiety on him because he cares for you...And the God of all grace, who called you to his eternal glory in Christ, after you have suffered a little while, will himself restore you and make you strong, firm and steadfast." 1 Peter 5:6-7, 10

Papa was our name for him. We had to ask him before we could do anything, but he asked, "What did your grandma say?" We knew Grandma had the final say, but we still had to go to him first. Papa was quiet for the most part. He truly had some struggles in life, like we all had/have. He too was a fallen saint. He dropped out of school and went to work to help his family. He only had a third-grade education. So, Grandma had to help with paperwork and everything else. My grandfather's vision wasn't the best. However, somehow, he had his license to drive. He took me to school for a couple of years while I was in elementary school. There wasn't a morning that went by that he wouldn't hit a trashcan.

I said, "Papa, you hit that trashcan."

He said, "It should get out the way."

You could either laugh or close your eyes. For me, I closed my eyes, held on to my seatbelt, and shook my head.

Then I asked for extra money for snacks. LOL. He gave it to keep me quiet because he knew I would tell Grandma, he hit the trashcans again. LOL.

My first heartfelt memory of my grandfather was the morning of my fifth-grade year. I went to get extra money for snacks. He was on the floor, but he wasn't laid out on the floor. He looked as if he was praying. So I went in the living room and asked Grandma why Grandpa was on the floor. Grandma rushed back to his room and yelled, "Call 911, call 911 **now**!" My heart rate went up tremendously and my tears were like a waterfall. If I would have known he wasn't praying, I could have done something.

I remember he was in the hospital for a while, but he thanked me for coming in to get that snack money. From that moment, my grandpa changed a lot. He stopped drinking, smoking, and he was extremely quiet most of the time. With three deaths in the past three years, it made me weary of who would be next. But like death, you never knew and never saw it coming. So, his death took me by surprise. I knew he had problems with breathing. He smoked for years, and I just figured that was the reason. A weekend before he went into the hospital, he was in his recliner, and he could not stop coughing.

He finally said, "I don't think I'm going to be here too much longer."

My grandma said, "Bo, you need to stop that. You know better than that."

He said, "I'm serious, I don't think I will be here much longer, you need to call my brother."

I'm not sure what transpired after that. I looked at him for a few minutes and my eyes filled with tears. Would he be next? What would we do? Why did everyone keep dying? Days passed and I thought nothing else about it. Until he was rushed to the hospital. He just couldn't breathe. They transported him to another hospital, and I just didn't feel confident that he would come home. As they took him out on the stretcher, my eyes filled with tears. I couldn't hold back my tears. I was so angry with God already because He took three good men from me. Three men who supported me. Would He take my grandpa, too? I felt childlike, helpless, small, afraid, and vulnerable. I'm not sure who it was this time, but someone in the family held me tightly and said, "He will be all right."

Later that night, my aunt Kay returned from the hospital and said, "Keisha, Papa told me to tell you he will be fine, he promised, so don't worry."

I didn't believe it, though. Either the past experiences or just intuition, I just didn't believe it. I'm not sure if it was the night he went to the hospital or the following day. But I was in the car with my boyfriend. We saw a car rush by as my mother walked toward me.

I said, "Something is wrong, I know it."

I got out of the car and she said, "Baby, Grandpa died."

"Noooooooooo! He promised, he promised he would come home. He promised, Mama, he promised." I cried and cried, and the next thing I remember was my eyes opened, and I was on the sofa. I had fainted. I just couldn't handle it.

Truthfully, I can't recall the events after this. They're blocked and I don't understand why. I want to wait to see if they will come to me, but I don't feel they will. So, I say this: My grandfather placed a strong impact on my life. He would be very proud of me, I am sure of it. God and I were not on good terms. I was so angry and hurt. I didn't go to church, pray, or anything else that had God in it. My senior year, my grandfather did not see me graduate. I headed to college with so much emptiness. I left family at home, my family left me on earth, I was just disgusted.

> *"I am worn out from my groaning.*
> *All night long I flood my bed with weeping*
> *and drench my couch with tears.*
> *My eyes grow weak with sorrow;*
> *they fail because of all my foes". Psalm 6:6-7*

> *"Why Lord do you stand far off? Why do you*
> *hide yourself in times of trouble?" Psalm 10:1*

> *"Hear my cry, O God;*
> *listen to my prayer.*
> *From the ends of the earth I call to you,*
> *I call as my heart grows faint;*

lead me to the rock that is higher than I"
Psalm 61:1-2

"Be merciful to me, Lord, for I am in distress;
my eyes grow weak with sorrow,
my soul and body with grief.
My life is consumed by anguish
and my years by groaning;
my strength fails because of my affliction,
and my bones grow weak". Psalm 31:9-10

"There is a time for everything, and a season
for every activity under the heavens: a time
to be born and a time to die, a time to plant
and a time to uproot...a time to tear down
and a time to build, a time to weep and a
time to laugh, a time to mourn and a time
to dance." Ecclesiastes 3:1-4

When Lord, when will I find joy again?...

Chapter Three

MOTHERHOOD...IT TAKES A VILLAGE

*"Before I formed you in the womb I knew
you, before you were born I set you apart;
I appointed you as a prophet to the nation".
Jeremiah 1:5*

*"If you are Christ's, then you are Abraham's
seed, and heirs according to the promise."
Galatians 3:29*

*"No in all these things we are more than
conquerors through Him who loved us."
Romans 8:37*

"Just go into your closet, baby, and give it to God." That would be Bernice, my mother. It wasn't until I became a mother that my closet began to mean more than a place to put my shoes and clothes. My prayer life and faith began to strengthen and progress during my motherhood walk. I prayed about many things. How would I carry this child and protect this child? Then, how would I guide this child? How would I pay these bills, go back for my master's, and raise my son? I prayed, but still I worried, but as I worried, I prayed. **But** I never wondered how I would love him. I felt that from the very start. Here comes my JOY...

This journey was through my motherhood vision. I was thankful to his dad/Pops for his help and support. His grandmothers who guided him, spoke with him about God, laughed, played, and drove him and his friends to games and practices. His aunts who supported him, made sure he had what he needed, fed and clothed him, and loved him unconditionally. His uncle for the "male time" bonding, summer trips, and constant understanding. As well as the rest of our family. Below are extra people God placed in our paths.

Motherhood, I thought, was just about loving and playing with your baby. **Wrong!** Motherhood goes deep within your soul to develop a fighter, protector, defender, unstoppable, phenomenal woman. When I say motherhood is **war,** oh, I have **battle scars**. Motherhood is filled with blood, sweat, tears, sleepless nights, weight of the world on my shoulders, heartaches, and pain. My journey did not come with a road map. I learned by trial and error, mistake after mistake. Or was it just me and mine? Still, I believe it's what you need to raise a humble, joyful, loving, patient, kind, gentle, faithful, good, and self-controlled young man like Xavier.

Xavier, my birthday baby, a fight I would cherish for all of my life. I wanted kids and when Xavier came along, I was scared. I didn't have much money. I did have my own home, car, and a job. Some said, "That's a good start." I felt I wasn't ready financially, but God... I remember my first Mother's Day. Xavier was still in the womb and I was at my computer and a song came on, *Alabaster Box*. Oh, this song would be the song I reached back for during my challenging motherhood moments and say, "God, only **You** know."

Oh, how Xavier has grown, from forty-two weeks and five days in the womb to twenty years old on earth. He was quiet, only kicking when he was hungry or too much noise was around. Xavier was due on October 9, 2000, but he just wasn't ready.

My grandma said, "Keisha, you can't rush that baby, he will come when the Good Lord wants him to come."

I worked as a behavioral analyst. I was tired of hearing the housekeepers ask, "You ain't dropped yet?"

"Ain't dropped what? I'm not an animal." I worked up until I was forty weeks. I couldn't see my feet, my stomach blew up overnight. I couldn't sleep or get comfortable. Lawd, I couldn't walk without pain, Jesus Father, was he making his way out, what was really going on down there? Pressure, pain, exhaustion, but **God!** Well, Xavier made his big entrance on October 14, 2000, and it was the best birthday present I could ever receive.

"and LaQuisha said to him, "Pardon me, my lord. As surely as you live, I am the woman who stood here beside you praying to the Lord. I prayed for this child, and the Lord has granted me what I asked of him. So now I give Xavier to the Lord. For his whole life Xavier will be given over to the Lord." And he worshiped the Lord there..."
1 Samuel 1:26-28

"And we know that in all things God works for the good of those who love him, who have been called according to his purpose. For those God foreknew he also predestined to be conformed to the image of his Son, that he might be the firstborn among many brothers and sisters. And those he predestined, he also called; those he called, he also justified; those he justified, he also glorified". Romans 8:28-30

Xavier was a very good kid. As I said, he didn't come with instructions. For example, it was very difficult for **me** to potty train him. Well, one Sunday afternoon, I was on the phone with my mother. Xavier and I were on the sofa.

Xavier said, "Pee-pee, Mommy, pee-pee." He ran to the bathroom and I waited at the door. I heard Xavier say, "Pee-pee come out, don't be scared, don't be scared. Zay, Zay here."

My mother said, "Is he talking to his pee?"

"Yes, ma'am."

Then we heard the perfect sound of the flow going into the toilet and Xavier said, "Good job." It was truly a moment of laughter, but we were so very proud of him.

Another moment, Xavier was around three or four. He would run up and down the stairs.

I said, "Xavier, don't you run on those stairs, you will get hurt."

So, one day, Xavier was downstairs in the den. I went upstairs to get something and came back downstairs (didn't run) but I slipped down the stairs. Xavier ran to the stairs and said, "Mommy, are you okay?"

I said, "Yes Xavier, Mommy's okay."

Xavier calmly and seriously said, "I told you not to run down dem stairs, you can get hurt" and he walked off. He didn't laugh, wasn't getting smart. He applied what I told him to the situation. I shook my head and laughed.

This time, Xavier was around four-and-a-half and played soccer. He was on the field doing what boys do at that age, dug in every hole he had, LOL and played in the dirt. Made a hole in the field LOL. Well, I had his folding chair out with an umbrella attached because I knew the heat would come. As the game started, the temp increased. I looked up, Xavier was in his chair, legs crossed like an old black man with a Gatorade in his hand.

The coach's wife said, "Xavier, honey, are you going back out there?"

33

Xavier kindly said, "No, Ma'am it's **hot!** He put on his shades and took his snack and drink.

Again, all I did was look, shake my head, and laugh softly.

This last one, Xavier may have been in the second or third grade. I was on Xavier about not studying his sight words. I spoke to Xavier about being a young man of his word. Meaning: Do what you say you are going to do, and if you can't, let people know. Well, Xavier seemed to be into the TV instead of his spelling words.

I asked, "Xavier, do you know those words?"

"Yes, ma'am."

"Okay, tomorrow I will find out, so is that your **word**?"

"Yes ma'am," Xavier said.

Well, the next day, I looked out the window and Xavier bopped into the house. He said repeatedly, "I'm a man of my word, I'm a man of my word." He came into the house, and he said, "Mommy, here is my spelling test." He was calm and confident.

I said, "Xavier what did you get?"

As he handed me the test, he said, "See, I am a man of my word," and walked off. No laughter, no smart mouth. Again, I shook my head and smiled, another proud moment.

As Xavier grew, he was the same way. He applied what you told him to a situation, which made me say, "See how it comes back on you?" LOL. He did not like chaos and confusion. His heart was on his sleeve. Xavier was and is truly the fruit of the Spirit. Each time you were in his presence, you would see it. For me, it was his smile. Oh how I loved and still love to see those "pearly white teeth." It was something about his smile that made my world all right again. Regardless of what it was, Xavier's smile was God's presence. There was a peace within Xavier only God created in him.

Xavier was a young man who was quick to listen, slow to speak, and slow to anger. He was a gentle giant. Regardless of his size or age, he was my baby boy. My heavenly Father got us through some rough, tough, some not so sure times, some heartaches and heartbreaks. Some tears, sleepless nights, some stress and worries, but in it we both became stronger, wiser, better, trusted, and knew God would see us through it. I strongly believed with everything in my heart God created Xavier for me, not me for him. I felt stronger more confident than ever before.

Motherhood did that. Xavier brought the mother lion out of me. I was his strongest advocate and critic, and when it came to sports, Mama was all over it. God brought special coaches into Xavier's path who taught him and saw his worth. Truth, not all the coaches had that, but still there were a few.

There was a moment Xavier was on the baseball field. He was in the third or fourth grade. As he ran to second base, the coach from the other team ran out behind him and said, "Who's this boy's mama?" I immediately stood up, wondering what happened, because he didn't seem like he was hurt. The coach yelled, "I need this boy on my football team. See me after the game."

We did go and Xavier wanted to play badly, and the coach wanted him on the team. Well, as I watched the coach, I realized he thought Xavier had this anger and rage inside of him. Not sure why. As I watched Xavier practice, I waited.

The first day they received their gear, the coach popped on a helmet and yelled, "X-Man hit that man!"

Xavier said, "No sir."

Coach pulled Xavier by the face mask and said, "Son, I said hit that man."

Xavier said, "No sir."

Coach said, "X, take off."

Xavier said, "Yes sir." He didn't complain, no anger, kindly ran his laps, and returned to the coach.

Coach said, "X-Man, I want you to hit that man."

Xavier said, "No sir, coach."

"X-Man why won't you hit this man?"

Xavier said, "Because he is too small, coach."

I smiled and shrugged my arms at the coach. I said, "He's not that kid, coach."

After practice, coach said, "X-Man has a good size on him. If I could just get him tough and hungry, he would be a beast."

I said, "Coach, Xavier has no need to be angry and I feed him regularly, so he will never be that hungry."

He laughed and shook his head, and said, "I see where he gets it from."

I knew what he meant, but he couldn't force Xavier to be what he was not. I knew the game a little, but it wasn't worth it. This was a little football league. He played, just not the "center" position, and Xavier was fine with it and his mother was too. LOL.

Xavier also played baseball. He never liked it, but since I liked softball, I knew it was something I could teach him. I knew it was something that would keep him busy. We tried to be placed on Coach Phil's team for years, and finally there was a spot. Xavier had played a couple of years prior. Well, he improved, and they made it to the championship. Xavier was on defense, third base, and his old football and basketball coach, Maurice was the coach for the other team and stood on first base. Xavier had never played infield before, but there weren't enough players, so players were moved around. The ball was hit, and it was thrown to Xavier to tag the person out at third. Xavier stood in the baseline and the player and Xavier collided. Luckily, no one was hurt, but Coach Maurice ran to Xavier, Coach Phil also. I stood there by the fence with my heart on the ground and my tears in my eyes.

Xavier stood up and said, "I'm good, coach."

Coach Maurice looked up at me, nodded, and smiled to reassure me. Coach Phil moved Xavier from third to left field (the position). I could see the disappointment in Xavier's posture as he walked out into the outfield. So, as I yelled his name to cheer him on.

Coach Phil yelled, "Guys, two outs any base, Xavier be ready." If the other team scored, they would be the champs. The pitch went and the ball was hit in the air. It went into the outfield, **Left** field!

I stood up and said softly to myself, "You got it, Xavier, you got it, Xavier, and Lord help him." Xavier's first move was a jump step, then a step forward, then dropped a leg back, and found the ball in the air and he **caught it**! Coach Maurice jumped up and down with joy and forgot Xavier was on the other team. Xavier ran the ball in as the players ran to him with excitement.

Coach Phil said with a deep voice, "This was why I put you out there, son."

Xavier said, "You believed in me, coach?"

"Yes, son I did," replied Coach Phil. It truly did his heart good to hear Coach Phil say that to him.

Xavier went from recreational ball to school ball. Mr. Walker was the athletic director at a charter school. Xavier was headed to the sixth grade, and once his foot hit the pavement, Mr. Walker said, "Hey son, you playing basketball this year, right?"

Xavier looked at him like, "Sir, this is my first day, I don't know."

I said, "Sorry, sir, Xavier is in the sixth grade."

Mr. Walker said, "He can play, just try out." This was the moment that started a beautiful relationship. Every morning before school, I dropped Xavier off and Mr.

Walker stood at the front door. He could see uniforms hung up in the back of my car.

One day he stopped me and asked, "How many sports does Xavier play?"

I said, "Four, but he only really likes one."

Later basketball tryouts began, but Xavier was still playing baseball for a recreational league. I told Mr. Walker because he would need to leave the tryouts early, but I didn't want to keep him from making the team.

Mr. Walker said, "Mom, you remind me of my mama. My mom went with us all over to play ball. Oh, by the way, Xavier is already on the team, just don't tell him that." I was so excited and proud, my eyes filled with tears. "Mom, you truly are like my mom. She did the same thing, tears of joy."

As Xavier changed into his uniform, I thanked Mr. Walker. Xavier and I ran up the walkway, I threw a piece of banana in his mouth as he ran and stuffed his shirt in his pants. I had a water and banana in one hand and his book bag in the other hand. We did this three days straight because he was in the semifinals with Coach Charles and Coach Maurice.

Mr. Walker instilled a lot of wisdom into Xavier. He joked with him a lot about being a "mama's boy." He then said, "Xavier, there's nothing wrong with being a mama's boy. I still am." Mr. Walker was a great man, miss him a lot.

Coach Anthony was the coach who started us off with AAU basketball. Xavier had finished up a church league and school ball wasn't that intense. Xavier wanted to play more, so I found a team. The tryouts were that night and we were late. From the moment Xavier's foot stepped on the court, Coach Anthony called his name. He continued to call his name throughout the entire tryout. Xavier was tired, but he did not stop running. It wasn't a fast run, more like a very light jog/trot. LOL. Well, he made the team, and the practice started. Xavier was accustomed to simple practice, not drills and plays. I was confused myself and wondered, "What did I get my son into?" Xavier looked at me like, "What has Mama gotten me into?" I asked Coach Anthony about every drill and every play. He told me not to worry, half of the things they wouldn't remember. Well, the first game, I pulled Xavier aside and we prayed.

Then I said, "Xavier, I know this team is new and the players are new, but basketball is basketball, son. Don't let it scare you because these people are loud and rude. Play your game, son, and I promise you will see that ball is ball." I saw the nervousness and I had it too because I wanted to see what I knew he could do, **play basketball**.

Well, before the game, Coach Anthony said to the team and parents, "I have a strong feeling someone is going to show me something different. I have a strong feeling someone is going to show up and show out today. I got a strong feeling I know who this someone is."

I heard him all the while I'm thinking, "My baby will show you." I wasn't sure if he was talking about X or not. Xavier was not in the starting five, and if you knew me, I didn't like that at all, because I knew he deserved to be there, he was just nervous. So the game started and then he called Xavier's name to check into the game. "Lord, once he gets a shot, he will be fine," I said aloud as I stood by myself in the stands.

A couple of trips up and down the court, someone threw Xavier the ball and he scored. **Again**, if you knew me, trust I didn't let you down. I screamed so loud I'm sure the devil was tired of my mouth. Oh, I was **loud** for my baby. Every time he scored, I called him by his last name, then I heard Coach Anthony call him by his last name and he never stopped calling his name.

Coach Anthony pulled Xavier aside and said, "I told you someone would show up and show out." This too was the start of a great relationship.

Coach Dwayne's son was also on the team, but I heard Coach Dwayne was a trainer. So I asked if he could train Xavier, because I knew Xavier needed some help with certain things. And did he ever. Coach Dwayne showed Xavier how to do a "hook shot." Man, he returned to the game and Coach Anthony was like, "Okay, Mom, who has been working with my man?" I pointed to Coach Dwayne. Xavier's game improved as well as his confidence.

You know what my first love was? **Basketball!** After the season and for a few summers after, Coach Dwayne picked up Xavier during the summer to help him and his son with basketball camps. He took them fishing, to his mother's home, and hung out with coach's wife and son. Once more, the start of a great relationship.

Coach Charles was Xavier's baseball coach, but we all met on a football field. Coach Charles, his wife, and son were very kind to Xavier and me. Coach Charles said he would teach Xavier a few things about baseball, and he did. He showed Xavier a lot of defensive moves and hitting techniques. Coach Charles spoke to the guys like he would his own son. I respected that completely. One game, Xavier just didn't swing the bat quick enough, and he was frustrated. Coach Charles pulled him aside and whispered something in his ear. Xavier went up to the home plate. Coach said, "X, move up, keep going and remember what I told you." There was the pitch and X hit the ball and made it to second base. Those types of moments stuck out to me. He continued to keep in contact with us to check on Xavier's progress.

There were moments throughout Xavier's high school years when I knew God would show up, I just didn't know how. Xavier played several sports all throughout school: soccer, basketball, football, baseball, lacrosse, and even ran cross country once (did very well). Still, basketball was his passion. I had that same desire as he did. God always brought someone who would be that "special person" to go alongside Xavier for encouragement. I just didn't know who it would be this time.

Coach Willie, now "Unk" as Xavier would and still calls him, started with us at a church league. It was mostly to keep that basketball in Xavier's hands. Well, coach and his beautiful wife took Xavier as their own. Xavier came home one day and said, "Uncle Willie and I are going to see a game."

I said, "Who is Uncle Willie?"

Xavier said, "Coach, mom."

I said, "Ooookay," and kept it moving.

The next day, I got a call from Coach Willie and he said, "Hey, Mom, how are you? Me and my wife talked last night and we would like for Xavier to come with us to the beach because he's like family to us."

I laughed and coach was like, "What's funny?" I said, "Xavier just called you uncle last night and I had no idea who Uncle Willie was."

Coach Willie quickly said, "Oh, X's my dude, so can he come?"

I said, "Yes."

Well, Coach Willie would pick Xavier up on weekends to go play pick up ball. Xavier didn't want me to go. For the first time, I saw Xavier making his way, and I was proud. It gave me time to just rest and I knew he was in good hands. Xavier, Coach Willie and his family had good times together during his high school years. So much so, Xavier will go by coach's house and visit whenever he is in Charlotte. "Mom, Unk said, 'Hey.'" Every once in a while, I would get a text from Coach: "Hey sis, just checking on my man X."

I wanted Xavier's basketball game to expand, and God sent us Coach Hasan. Coach Hasan came along during a summer I wanted Xavier's game to excel on what Coach

Dwayne had instilled in him. Well, Coach Hasan worked with Xavier. That first workout, I was like, "I don't know about this, it's intense," and there were professional ball players with him. Xavier loved it and soon he caught on to the drills and worked with Coach Hasan more and more. Coach improved Xavier's ball handling skills. It opened Xavier's eyes to wanting to play on the wing instead of the inside. Coach Hasan helped Xavier to get a spot at the basketball camp at UNC Chapel with Kenny Smith.

Okay, I had to share this because I was so super excited and proud of Xavier, but his response was totally different. After Xavier returned from the camp, which was I think a week (Side note: if you knew me, you knew I cried like a big baby because he was not with me), I said, "How was the camp?"

Xavier said, "Good." He doesn't really show excitement. So, I asked question after question, nothing from Xavier. Two days later, I received a few pictures from the camp. Xavier had a picture with Kenny Smith. I was like, "OMG, my baby, look at my baby!"

Xavier said, "Oh, I forgot I took that picture," and went on about his way.

Again, I shook my head and laughed softly. We were and are so grateful to have Coach Hasan. His favorite line to Xavier was, "Good Stuff, X!"

And then God sent us three more: Coach Will, Teddy, and Sam came along at the same time. Another AAU team, but we felt like we had always been on the team. Coach

Teddy was the first coach we met during tryouts for another AAU team. Xavier's nervousness didn't show, still I knew he was just a little.

Coach Teddy said immediately, "He has a different type of game, I like it, but I don't make the decision."

Coach Will walked in with his earpiece in his ear. I remembered him from previous years. You never realize how God places people in your path.

"Hello Coach, I'm Keisha and this is Xavier."

Coach Will spoke and then said, "Let me see what you got." Coach later said, "I like the way he plays, but I'm not sure if there will be room on the team for him, we've started playing."

I said, "We will be fine, he just wants to play, coach."

There was a game that same weekend. Coach said, "Have him here and we will get him a ride."

I said, "I'm his ride, I travel with my son."

Coach quickly said, "Oh, you're that kind of mom, I like that." From that moment, Coach Willie and his wife Kim made us feel so welcomed. Wherever the team went, I was right there and began to grab a player or two to help. Then Xavier began to work with Coach Sam (Coach Teddy's twin brother) from time to time. I'm not sure what was said, but I knew Xavier respected Coach Sam. He spoke very highly of him, Coach Teddy, and Coach Will. All three coaches gave Xavier something different, but they all gave him something he could carry with him for the remainder of his life.

During Xavier's junior year in high school, he fractured his ankle. I was devastated, because Xavier worked so hard all summer. I prayed more than I had ever before. "Lord, why? Please don't let this be like my high school years." Okay, first this was not about me, so get out your feelings "**LaQuisha!**"

Xavier was in pain as I took him to the doctor. When we received the news that it was fractured, I thought he would be more devastated, but he said, "God has a plan, Mom, don't worry." He could see it on my face. I was just so hurt, but I'm sure he was too and didn't want me to see it. I understood, I went through it, but once again, "**Quisha, get out your feelings!**" Xavier went through the process and he went to practice every day and on time. He was at every game, and I sat in the stands with the stink face. I had to really go into prayer and ask for forgiveness. This happened to my son who handled it very well. I had to go back into that closet and get myself together.

The summer before his senior year, Xavier worked with a trainer, Hunter. He spoke life into Xavier. It wasn't just about his body, it was about his mind, his soul, his future, and how to be a good man. Oh, how I hated to see Hunter move from Charlotte. Still, he gave Xavier things he still uses today. You recall me asking earlier, "Lord, when will Xavier receive his moment?" Well, Xavier's senior year, he received several opportunities to play basketball and was crowned "King" at the prom. Many of his coaches, along with family, attended the signing day (Coach Maurice,

Willie, Will, and Bobby). I had a friend to say, "God is showing you glimpses of his future." Xavier had his arms around my mother and me, and family were behind us after he "signed" his commitment papers to a college. He made the decision and I respected it. However, I wasn't ready for him to leave.

The day of his graduation, I woke up at 6 am. I went for a walk. As I started the walk, I realized Xavier was really leaving. Tears ran down my face. "Lord, what do I do now?" I cried for about an hour and realized I had completed my walk. I couldn't get myself together, I had emotions after emotions. I remembered Xavier was there when I graduated with my master's degree. I remembered Xavier was there when I got baptized. I recalled he was right there when I received my grief counselor certificate. We have truly been cheerleaders for each other. The family was ready, Xavier was really ready, but his **mother** not so much.

As he walked down the aisle, the graduation song played. My tears began. "Lord, how am I going to make it through this graduation?" I could see him looking around, but I "his mama" was straight ahead. "Xavier, baby." He smiled and said, "Hey, Mom." When they called my son's name, I stood up, but I couldn't yell loud because I cried too hard. I needed to capture the moment he walked across that stage. It brought back the moments of hard work, prayers, and talks with teachers to make sure they were doing their jobs. I could hear my baby sister, Nikki, out of all the screams, so I didn't need to yell. My mom stood beside me with joy on her face.

I just couldn't believe how time went so fast and he grew into a wonderful young man. He did his dance and walked across that stage with **pride**. In that moment, I thought back to the times of getting him up early to get to work, taking him to UNC Charlotte classrooms and library as I worked hard to receive my master's degree. I recall the nights I watched him as his fever would not break. When he worked so hard in school. He walked across that stage and all I said was, "Look at You, God."

That's what I placed on my Spiritual Resume. **"Growth!"** You see, it took me a long time to realize this journey wasn't because "I" got myself through it. I reached a level of spiritual maturity this was **God**. It took time, but God knew time was what I need and needed. I'm so glad Shay and Joann came to graduation, because they filmed it and my Uncle Dan and Jeanette filmed. After graduation, I saw our family, friends, his friends, but I didn't see my son. Where was my son? As I laid eyes on him, he walked toward me, arms long and wide, teeth pretty and white, smile big as the sun. I hugged my baby boy with tears in my eyes. I was so tremendously proud of him.

Xavier said, "We did it, Mom, we did it."

We collected ourselves and saw two familiar faces, Coach Teddy and Coach Sam. Xavier was so happy to see them there. After the pictures, I realized my feelings resurfaced. **"I'm not ready for him to leave!"** Who would I wait on until 9:30pm but say I stayed up till 11pm, waiting on him to come home? I left my door open and he would come into my room and say, "Mom, I'm home." Well, I was a trooper for about a month and I couldn't hold on any more. I would close my eyes and could feel something wet on my forehead, but I never opened my eyes. Whenever I woke up, usually around 2 am, I would see my door closed. I knew the wet feeling on my forehead. It was always Xavier. He would come in, cover me up, kiss me on my forehead, and close the door. Who would do this now? What about the sound of the microwave in the middle of the night? Or the squeaking of sneakers on a court and a coach yelling because he watched film all night, and if I turned it off he woke up and said, "I'm listening to it, Mom." Who would do this now?

Still, I felt I prepared Xavier for his independence and college. He knew how to wash his clothes, basic cleaning, and to be responsible or consequences would follow. I knew he would have to figure things out on his own, but he had the tools he needed to do so. Still, I felt I didn't prepare myself. I struggled hard. For me, I had placed **all** of me into my motherhood journey. I had moments of good and bad, but I grew as a person, as a woman, because of God and Xavier. So, what would I do now that he was gone? Yes, I would always be his mother, and as his mother I must allow him to experience life for himself. This meant he would make mistakes, have heartbreaks, sadness, and pain, but he had that before and God got him through it. He would have victories, accomplishments, the love of his life, family, wealth, joy, peace, good health, but most of all **faith**. I sat in the "empty nest" for a moment. I refused to rush myself out of it because I needed to be sure I felt whatever I wanted and needed to feel. So I did, and then I began to work on me.

In the moments of working on me, I still found myself thinking about those who helped along the way. I recalled Dr. Jones, who guided me on the journey of UNDERSTANDING and RAISING a teenage boy. He also helped me to prepare for each year of Xavier's middle and high school years. He was always right.

A few weeks after Xavier left, I was in my office late. Dr Jones walked by and said, "Why are you still here?"

I softly said, "I don't have anywhere to go anymore, my son is gone." In that moment, he saw my pain and I knew he could hear the cry in my voice. I fought back the tears, but my heart cried.

Dr. Jones began to tell me his journey of dealing with an empty nest. It brought me comfort and I was always grateful for him, for the time he took to speak with me. He has always felt like an older big brother.

Big brother: that reminds me of Chris L. He came into our life as a representative for an agency. Neither one of us would imagine he would be called Uncle Chris L by Xavier and Big Bro by me. He allowed me to express my thoughts and feelings. He listened and gave advice. I listened and gave him advice. The thing was, he truly does feel like my brother. Our birthdays are a day apart. It's like we were separated at birth. He took Xavier aside and away from me a few times after a game and a weekend, to just talk to him "uncle talk," he said. Xavier said, "Mom, Unk is a cool dude."

Then I thought of Dr Price, who took time out to look at Xavier's ankle, shoulder, etc. He would always ask, "How's Xavier?" He never said, "Quisha, I don't have time." He listened and gave feedback: ice, elevate, rest!

Dr Martin introduced Xavier to Hunter. He also helped Xavier with his prom outfit for his senior year. Xavier would send a pic and I took it to Dr. Martin. That went on for a few days. LOL.

I won't forget the extended family members: Miss Teresa, Miss Venette, Tasha, Karen H, Sam, Davida, Tonya, Tonya R, Verna, Victoria, Mrs. Linda, Mrs. Sarah (birthday buddies) Katherine, Dr. Menscer, Dr. Carr, Dr. Culpepper, Stephanie, Hakyma, Ambra, Sandra V, Sandra T, Jill, Carla, Phyllis, Casandra, Angela, Josette, Bethany, Will, and others who played a part in my son's life. We cannot forget adopted Auntie Joann, Erica, Shaneek, Kia, and Shay. Those men who watched Xavier, picked him up when I couldn't find anyone, thank you Fretral and Marcus.

I placed expectations on Xavier since he was a child. I wanted him to be a child of God, to believe in Him and what He said He would do. I expected Xavier to treat others like he wanted to be treated. I expected Xavier not to be taken advantage of and to understand he couldn't help everybody. Well, I should've expected that for myself, but you always want better for your children. Xavier felt at times I was too hard on him. As I look back, I was, but with reasons.

I made many mistakes along the way, but I know what I know. I put Xavier at the forefront each and every time. So I went to him with folders, labeled with each scholarship I had applied for that I knew he deserved. As he looked at me, I let him know I loved him. Then I said, "Xavier, where are you going?"

He said, "College."

I asked, "What are you going to do in college?"

He said, "To play basketball and get a degree."

I said, "You see my point. I knew and know you have greatness in you, son. I know you can because God has shown me. Trust, son, you leaving hurts me more than you will ever know, but it will hurt you and me more if you stayed home. My expectations were to encourage you and it did. You are someone that everyone comes to for advice, the coaches can depend on you to do the right thing. You are a joy to be around. You help people and try to do the things you promise. You are a young man who speaks God's words and knows where your help comes from. You treat others like you want to be treated. You love those who wronged you. See, son, you met and exceeded my expectations already at eighteen. So now this was what I knew you could do."

"She opens her mouth with wisdom, And the teaching of kindness is on her tongue." Proverbs 31:26 NASB

It was time and Xavier entered another stage of his life and I was right there. We came across Coach Houck and what a relief I had after speaking with him. Anyone who knew me knew, **I ask questions.** LOL. Coach Houck answered every question and gave me his phone number in case I had more. Coach Houck spoke the word of God in his life and to the other young men. For me as a praying mother, that means a great deal. Give me a praying man and coach any day, I will take and accept him, Lord.

There were many times in my prayer closet, I wrote down scriptures circling Xavier.

> *"So do not fear, for I am with you; do not be dismayed, for I am your God. I will strengthen you and help you, I will uphold you with my righteous right hand." Isaiah 41:10*

> *"My flesh in my heart may fail, but God is the strength of my heart in my portion forever." Psalm 73:26*

> *"I can do all things through Christ who strengthens me." Philippians 4:13*

> *"He gives strength to the weary and increases the power of the weak." Isaiah 40:29*

"Give me a sign of your goodness, that my enemies may see it and be put to shame, for you, Lord have helped me and comfort me." Psalm 86:17

"Start children off on the way they should go, and even when they are old they will not turn from it". Proverbs 22:6

"For I know the plans I have for you, declares the Lord, plans to prosper you and not to harm you, plans to give you hope in a future." Jeremiah 29:11

"But now, this is what the Lord says he who created you, oh Jacob, he who formed you, or is real fear not, for I have redeemed you; I have summoned you by name; You are mine." Isaiah 43:1

"For he will command his angels concerning you to guard you in all your ways they will lift you up in their hands, so that you will not strike your foot against a stone." Psalm 91:11

"Because Xavier loves me, says the Lord, I will rescue Xavier; I will protect him, for he acknowledges my name. He will call upon me,

and I will answer him; I will be with Xavier in trouble, I will deliver him and honor him. With long life will I satisfy Xavier and show him my salvation." Psalm 91:14-16

"Have I not commanded you? Be strong and courageous. Do not be afraid; do not be discouraged, for the Lord your God will be with you wherever you go." Joshua 1:9

"The Lord will make you the head, not the tail. If you pay attention to the commands of the Lord your God that I give you this day and carefully follow them, you are always be at the top, never at the bottom." Deuteronomy 28:13

"For the Lord gives wisdom, from his mouth come knowledge and understanding." Proverbs 2:6

"Trust in the Lord with all your heart and lean not on your own understanding; in all your ways acknowledge him, and he will make your paths straight." Proverbs 2:5-6

"Let us not become weary in doing good, for at the proper time we will reap a harvest if we do not give up." Galatians 6:9

"but those who hope in the Lord will renew their strength. They will soar on wings like eagles; they will run and not grow weary, they will walk and not be faint." Isaiah 40:31

Chapter Four

GRANDMA, HOW I LOVE CALLING YOUR NAME

"She opens her hand to the poor and reaches out her hands to the needy. She is not afraid of snow for her household, for all her household are clothed in scarlet." Proverbs 31:20-21 ESV

Growing up, "Ma," "Grandma," "Catherine," "Aunt Little Liza," "Gal," and "Mrs. Catherine" were what you would hear before you opened your eyes and even after you closed them later. She had many names, but they all meant the same thing **Power, Respect, Wisdom, Lion, Warrior, Conqueror, Teacher, Preacher, Counselor, Doctor, Nurse, Chef, Fortune Teller,** and **Secret Keeper**. Ma displayed herself in a way I can't really describe. She knew things before they transpired. Ma could look at you and tell you that you were pregnant before you knew. She never valued things. She said, "Don't worship things, you can't take it with you." She also said, "You need to do it (whatever "it" was) yourself, you came in the world alone you will be buried alone."

Grandma, she made it all right again for me. If it bled, she cleaned it up; if it growled, she fed it; if it was disobedient, she gave a switch; if it was hurting, she gave her attention and advice. She had it all, one-stop shop. Ma could sew, cook, listen while asleep, and tell you what you needed to know with her eyes closed. As she said, "Every closed eye ain't asleep, just resting."

I stayed under my grandmother Catherine a lot. She was a force to be reckoned with. She stood tall, thick, quiet in nature, and when she spoke you stood still and at attention. She had wisdom, unexplainable knowledge for someone who did not finish school. There were times I came home from school only to find her in her recliner with an encyclopedia. She read them all the time. She loved history. My grandmother was slick with the tongue. Some may say this is where I get it from. Guess what? I don't mind it at all. She could advise you and tell you off all at the same time. You never saw it coming and you often scratched your head and would think to yourself, "Did she just tell me off in a nice, direct way?"

Yes, she had some amazing sayings that I never understood in the moment, but in time, it came to me. For instance, "Just keep on living." She said this a lot whenever we had hard times and wondered how we would get through them or over them. Things we experienced and didn't understand why they transpired like they did. "Just keep on living." Often times, we would get punished, but still didn't learn the lesson, "Just keep on living." Sometimes we were hurt by the ones we loved or betrayed by them as well. "Just keep on living." It was like she was saying, "You haven't seen or felt nothing yet." Boy, she was right.

The other saying was, "You keep ramming your head against that brick wall, and how is that working out for you?" This was when you tried to fix it and you tried it over and over again, but it never changed. You hurt yourself more and more, but you kept trying to fix it. "How is it working out for you?" she asked. Or she asked, "Has it moved yet?" I ran my head into many walls to only find I could never knock them down. Meaning, I had no control over the situation because it wasn't my task to obtain the "control," it was my job to be the vessel. Yes, you see, I have stood in God's way many times, not intentionally and not thinking or believing that I could do it better than God. However, I wanted that instant gratification. I wanted to be rid of the pain. Still, had I taken my hands off of it, the mess wouldn't have been a "foul mess." If I would've taken my hands off it, I could have been rid of it by now. If I took my hands off of it, my shoulders would be lighter. The weight that prevents me from standing strong, that's on me.

You see, I couldn't do anything without God. So, why do I forget this when my task is before me? I'm still a fallen saint. You see, He continues to work on me, in me, through me, and around me. Regardless of my mistakes, He knows my heart. He also knows how He has created me. This is why He keeps helping me, because God knows my intentions are pure.

Still my grandma would say, "Don't worry about the mule going blind, just sit back in the wagon and hold the line." This one was something she and my grandfather, Bo Martin would say. My grandmother watched my grandfather make mistakes in their marriage. I didn't hear her say too much, but of course in those days children were seen, not heard. In our household, not seen or heard in "grown folk business." We had to go outside (rain, snow, sleet, hail, heat) if there was ever a grownup conversation. So, whenever my grandfather forgot to pay a bill or didn't do anything, she would just look at him, but not say much. At least, not when we were around. I often wonder how she could get through those times without saying a word. "Just keep on living, she was finished ramming her head against a wall." It brought forth patience and resilience that was profound and glowed in her presence. She placed a mark on us all to the point we still call out her name now whenever we are troubled.

Time and time again, she gave us unconditional love. She was a pillar of spiritual strength for a woman who never went to church. She said, "God is everywhere and He is in me and as long as I call out to Him, He will answer." You know, I never saw her read the Bible, but I knew and never doubted she knew God. I never doubted it because she had a faith that was indescribable. She was remarkable in that way.

One of the sayings she had, I don't use at all because I knew she would pop me in my mouth from the grave, although she used it from time to time. "Speak when spoken to, come when you're called, you will make somebody a good old house dog." Jesus help the one who received that. I only heard her say that once, but it was a mouth dropped and eyes like a deer in headlights moment. She was upset, but she didn't raise her voice. She said it, and she moved on. The look she gave me was like, "Don't you dare repeat it." It was as if she knew it was wrong to say, but she said it because she was "hurt" and not heard. I don't use it, but it does come to mind at times. I smile and often laugh aloud, because it's so cutthroat you just can't use it. You know in your spirit and even in your flesh that's just not the thing to say.

My grandmother had many myths as well. They were funny, and we didn't believe them, but we would not try them either. LOL. For example, "If you cross water (bridge, lake, ocean, etc.) before your child was a month old, he/she would drool for the rest of his/her life." That one, I said, "Grandma, that's not true." However, when I had my son, I didn't come home until he was exactly a month old. It didn't sound right to me, but I wasn't going to go against what she said. I trusted her, I believed her, and never had she steered me wrong. Whenever our menstrual cycle was on, we could never open her freezer. She said, "You will spoil all my food." Or we couldn't wash our hair or get our hair wet because she said, "That will make your cramps stronger and your flow heavier." Now that I thought was true. That pain was something I won't forget.

"Never lift anything heavier than your child after birth until three months. Your body needs time to heal." She said, "Don't wash your hair until a month after childbirth because your pores are opened. It will increase your flow and cramps will be painful."

"Don't eat dairy and seafood during the same meal," it's truly not a good mixture. Shay, we can smile on that one lol.

I'm sure you are thinking what we thought, "Really, no way." When Grandma spoke, everyone listened. On Sunday mornings, she turned off all the TVs and she listened to the radio station play gospel music until noon. The house was quiet and she had her worship the entire time. She never sang aloud, shouted, or spoke in tongues. Grandma listened and felt whatever she needed to feel. Sometimes she was on the front porch with this white washing machine. It had a roller where you had to take one piece of clothing at a time and guide it through. The clothes would fall into the "wash tub" she had on the opposite side. Then we had to squeeze out the water from those clothes, guide them back through and put them in a basket for them to be hung on the clothesline. Yes I'm only forty-three. LOL. This was how we lived. Don't judge! All the time we did this, we couldn't say anything, because Grandma had to worship.

I strongly feel she was remembering her hard times from her childhood, like when her mother died. The times she buried her five sons. The pain she had was tremendous, but she stood strong on the battlefield of life. She had no doubt that God would see her through because He had proven time and time again, He was there for her.

My grandmother fed many, but I never saw her give money. She would say, "I can feed you a little, but I have a family of my own to feed. I won't give you money because you won't pay it back, and if I did you would blow it on something you don't need." She was very well respected and loved without measure. She had a way of being spiritually present, and I could hear her voice whenever I needed to. She was and is deep in my spirit and my soul. Grandma, Ma, Gal (she didn't like that my grandpa called her that). We called her so much, she knew it before we did. We got hurt outside, and before we could get the cry out good, she yelled, "Don't call my name, you should've sat your butt down." When we walked in the house, she said, "Don't call my name." All the while our thoughts were, "How did she know?"

Got your uniform, church shoes, needed answers, had a cough, an unidentified bump, scratch, or bruise, "Grandma, Ma." I would call and she listened, and was willing to say, "Well, here's my two cents. You didn't have to take it, but it would be crazy of you not to."

The moments of sitting under her as she sat on the sofa reading or completing a word find puzzle brought me joy. She sewed quilts for us for the winter, she canned food for the winter in the summer. She always seemed one step ahead. We never knew how she knew, but it was because "she kept on living" and we had just started. Now that she has passed, I will call out her name. I'm telling you, the wind will start to blow softly, the more I call out or cry, the stronger the wind will blow. That's Grandma, saying, "Keisha, don't cry yourself sick." She would never say not to cry, just not to cry yourself sick. Today, I get it. Crying too much, you lose something, you weaken your body, spirit, and your soul. Crying cleanses the body, I strongly believe, but too much you can lose yourself in those tears. It's hard to come back from, but with God it's possible to regain your strength with His strength. We would soon need it.

November 27, 2012, was unusual for me. I woke up and my phone was in the bed under the covers, with the screen completely black. I thought maybe I turned it off by mistake. Luckily, Jesus woke me up that morning because my alarm certainly didn't. Well, I tried many things: took the battery out, fussed, threw it aside and came back to it. It didn't matter, the Blackberry was dead. So I asked Xavier if I could use his phone for the day. As he said yes and handed it to me, I felt strange. Something within me just did not feel right.

Well as the day went on, this feeling became stronger, but I tried to ignore it because I had no idea what it was. I thought since my phone was not working, I was really feeling a certain type "a way about that thang." So I decided to go on about my day. I went to work and stayed in the office the majority of the time, because I tried to figure out whose numbers were in my son's phone. I had to let my sisters and mom know that I was using Xavier's phone.

Well, later that day, Xavier had a basketball game in Monroe. I tried and tried to get there as fast as I could without speeding. For some reason, my heart beat was fast, my hands shaky, and I could not figure out what was going on. I could not get it together, and once I turned onto the back road to get to the destination, my heart seemed as if it could jump smooth out of my chest. I immediately thought, "What is going on? **Am** I afraid of the dark and being on this back road by myself? Lord guide me." I called my sister Chris and explained to her what I felt. As she tried in her own way to let me know that I was crazy she talked about something else. As I reached the location, I was told that the game had not started, the referees were late. I saw Xavier and he realized that I was there. I was okay, but not really. After the game we had dinner, still I felt strange. We got home and ready for bed, still the feeling did not go away.

Xavier's cell phone rang. I thought, "Who is calling me at this time of night?" The screen showed it was Chris's fiancé (Mike), and I thought to myself, "I know that girl did not have this man to bring me a phone at this time of night." Something in me told me not to answer the phone. Then there was loud knock on the door and my heart started beating faster than before. I felt like I was in a scary movie, and I could see what was going to happen, but I had no way of stopping it. The loud knock came again as I ran downstairs. As I opened the door, the cell phone rang again upstairs. At the door was Mike, he was calling me from the front door. He was in his police uniform (the ironic thing was I had seen him many times in it), but my heart skipped a beat and I immediately became fearful. "Why would I be so afraid if I'd seen him in this before? Why did I want to drop to the floor and cry in this moment"?

So then he said, "Did someone call you?"

I said, "Yes, the phone just rang, but it's upstairs, what's wrong?"

His face was red and it seemed as if he wanted to cry. It seemed as if he had something to say and did not want to say it because then he would have to believe it for himself. He said, "It's Ma, her heart stopped."

Ma? Ma? My Ma? Grandma? I ran up those stairs and I just couldn't get dressed fast enough.

"Xavier, get up Xavier," I said. "Get up." I was in my room, trying to find anything to put on as I called out to Xavier, "**Get up**."

Well, he heard nothing. His door was closed, he was tired, and full all at the same time. I pushed his door opened turned on his light, and yelled, "**Xavier, get up!**"

He jumped up as if his heart was in his throat because of the fear of the unknown and my loud mouth. He ran in a circle because he was somehow still asleep, but knew that Mom was either scared or pissed off, it did not matter, he knew he had to spring into action. He got his clothes on and I said to him, "Something is wrong with Grandma, baby, we got to go now."

He immediately started to cry. In his mind, he thought it was his grandma, my mother. He asked what happened. I was confused, ran in a circle tried to find whatever I needed to find. I couldn't find it, so I decided to forget it.

We ran down the stairs and Mike said, "I was on my way to work and Mama called." I was pissed because Mama did not call me, but this was not the time. I would take care of that later. (You see, I'm always the last one to know about death in the family. My family feels they have to shield me.) Xavier was in the back crying and I was praying out loud, "Lord, help her to be okay. Lord, help her right now. Jesus, Jesus, please Jesus, don't. Please, not right now, Jesus, please."

Xavier then said, "Lord, please help my grandma, please Lord."

I turned back to him and said, "Baby, it's Nana, it's Nana." He screamed and said, "No not Nana, but I love her."

Mike's phone rang, and it was my mother. He said, "Okay, oh my God, oh no. Okay, okay."

I said, "Is she, is she, Mike?"

As he drove, his head dropped for a second. His face was red as well as his eyes. I saw the tears form in his eyes. My heart stopped. I couldn't breathe. Xavier screamed, "Noooooooooooooo!" and then I yelled as loud as I could.

I got on the phone and said, "Mama, you have to keep her there until I get there, you can't let them take her until I get there. Mama, please Mama, please."

She said in the voice that only she could have, soft and slow, "Okay baby, I promise.

This was the longest ride back to my sister's house. I cried, Xavier cried, Mike was quiet and wanted to cry. We prayed that it wasn't true, that it was possible they were able to revive her.

"Lord, what is going on? Lord, this is Grandma. Lord, please not now. Lord, please help her. Lord, help us. Lord, Lord, Lord." I continued saying this until we pulled in my sister's driveway.

Well to my surprise, my sister did not have any idea what was going on. Mike parked the car and looked at me and asked, "Do you want to tell her, or me? I shook my head. Mike dropped his head and said, "Okay, I will be back." Minutes later, I heard a loud scream, and as Xavier and I looked up, Chris ran without any shoes, socks, jacket, nothing. I opened the door and it seemed as if she leaped into my arms. She screamed a cry that I still can't get out of my head. She asked questions I did not have the answers to. She held me so tightly around my neck I could not get a breath or speak. I told her we needed to get her ready because we had to get there. We had to get there before they took Ma. Chris cried the entire ride. All I could do was follow the moon.

We got into Mount Gilead (our hometown) and Mike stepped on the gas pedal. He had his flashers on, my sister was on the horn the entire time, along with that whining cry she had. Xavier was frozen in the back because he did not know what was going on. It was too much for him. I looked out the window, prayed as I had the entire ride. As

Mike turned the curve, it was a straight shot to my aunt's house and all we could see were cars, lights, and people on both sides of the road.

Mike pulled over, but he had not stopped, the truck was still moving. It was as if my sister and I had the same thought and the same movement at the same time. I heard our seat belts click at same time, then the doors opened at the same time, we jumped out of the truck as it moved, at the same time. We took off running, and in the middle of the crowd I lost her. I couldn't figure out why my legs were moving, but I wasn't getting anywhere. I couldn't see Chris anymore. Where did she go?

I heard a loud voice say, "Calm down and I will put you down."

I swung in the air but missed whoever had me in the air. I heard a voice, the voice I'd heard for thirty-five years that could calm me and soothe me other than my grandma's voice. I heard, "Put her down." Yes indeed, it was Mama. She promised she would not let them take her until I got there. She promised and she kept that promise. I took off running again to try to get into the house, but Mama stopped me. She had me so tight. I couldn't move, she had that much of a handle on my arm.

I kept saying, "But Mama, you promised I would see her before they took her. Mama please, Mama please."

Mike went up to the other police officers and explained that we just drove from Charlotte and we wanted to see her.

As they pushed grandma out of the house on a strether, I said again, "Mama, you promised."

My mother said to Leroy (funeral home staff and a friend and church member), "Please let her see her."

As he pulled the zipper down from the black body bag, I said, "No, that's not her. Grandma, Ma, Ma," and there was no answer.

In that moment, that very moment, I saw her for the last time. Her mouth was twisted, her face was pale, no movement, no cussing, no fussing, it was just silence in my head in that moment. As he zipped the black dull body bag back up, I couldn't do anything but scream. I didn't know what more I could do but scream. I wanted her back. I wanted her well. I wanted the pain that she felt to not have occurred. "Lord, what happened? What happened?"

Family was leaving and we had just got there. I remembered hugs and kisses, but I couldn't recognize the voices because I just got there. I just got there and to me I just got there and everyone else had been there for a while and they were leaving. Still, I just got there. I wondered, cried, screamed, "What happened?"

As I cried, outside in the cold, Xavier said, "It's going to be okay, Mom." He hugged me, then my baby sister Nikki came and she sat down by my right knee, and here came Chris, cried that cry, hugged me as tight as she could.

My mother and my Auntie Janie (close friends but like sisters) were there, and Aunt Janie said, "Your girls are always there for each other, they are close, Bernice."

I guess in that moment my mother saw how distance could not divide us. As they left for a moment, my mother took me for a walk. She said, "Baby, it was just her time. I know you don't want to hear it, but Ma knew she was going to leave this world. She said to me, 'Bonnie, this is my last dinner.' I knew then something was wrong."

I said, "But mama, she would always say this was her last dinner cooking."

Mom said, "That's just it, she didn't say cooking, she said, 'This is my last dinner.'"

In that moment as we walked, I remembered last Thursday, which was Thanksgiving when I went to leave to go back to Charlotte. I said to Grandma, "Love you, Ma," and kissed her on her cheek. Well, out of all the years I had said that to her, she never said it back until then. In the moment I did pause, but did not do anything but smile. However, as my mother and I were walking, I realized that she was saying goodbye. I cried all over again, because I missed it. I didn't say anything, I didn't ask why she said it then in that moment when she had never said it before.

Who was going to pick up the pieces now? Who was going to take care of the family now? Who was going to make it right/whole again? Who would carry this burden as Ma had for eighty-five years? Who? Who?

The ride back to Charlotte was quiet. Not because we were done crying, but because we were numb. We were in shock, dismayed, somehow in disbelief that this was happening to us, to her. "Ma, Grandma is dead. Grandma is dead. Grandma is dead." No matter how many times you said it, "Grandma is dead," it did not sound right, it did not fit, and it did not register in my head that this was happening.

Mike pulled up to my house, Xavier and I got out, and my sister said, "I love you."

I hesitated. I did not want to say it back because I was fearful. "Are you telling me goodbye too? Is this your way of saying goodbye for good?" So I remember not repeating it. I said, "Me too," and dropped my head.

I heard Mike tell Xavier, "Take care of your mom, Zay."

He said, "Yes sir, I will."

As we went into the house, I told Xavier to go to bed. It was three in the morning. I couldn't sleep, I couldn't speak, I couldn't -- I just couldn't. As the sun came up, I wondered if maybe I was dreaming and I didn't realize it. So I ran upstairs to go to the bathroom, and I looked in the mirror as I went to brush my teeth. You know, it's amazing what your eyes or other people's eyes can tell you if you just look into them. My eyes were swollen from top to bottom. They were swollen, red, burning, and tired. This was when I realized that I wasn't dreaming.

Grandma was dead. The feeling that I felt all day Tuesday was because of Grandma. Was this God sending me a sign to let me know, "Something is going to happen beyond your control and you have to find a way to move through it and move forward"? I didn't have that feeling anymore, it was gone. It left once I was told that her heart stopped. All this time, it was Grandma and I did not know it. All this time I had a feeling that something was wrong, that something was just not right. All this time, it was **Grandma**.

I went to check in on Xavier and I realized that he was too tired and too hurt to go to school. So I called Mrs. Linda (a mother figure and friend), who immediately said, "Hey, Quisha, what's wrong, honey?" As she asked, I started crying all over again. Something about that question, or "How are you?" that will make you cry all over again. So I told her and she too was so surprised, she had a long pause. It reassured me of my feelings. She was my grandma, my Ma, but the reaction everyone else was giving was similar to mine at the time: **shocked, stunned, disbelief!**

I had to get her supervisor's number so I could get my supervisor's number because my phone still was not working. I called Will and said, "Will, my ..." and broke down in tears. I was broken, destroyed in a way that I could not see a rebuilt moment in my life. She was my foundation, she knew it all, and she could fix it even if it was unfixable. Why? Because she was Grandma. She was the hero without a cape, she was untouchable, unbeatable, and she was **Grandma**. She was the one who fed us, clothed us, made us laugh and cry, and made us well, because she was **Grandma**. No one could ever take her place, no one could ever do the things she did and how she did it because she was **Grandma**.

Will gave me that moment of silence, and he too was shocked. He told me to take all the time I needed, and if

I needed anything to call his cell. He had lost his grandmother that year. Well, after the calls, I realized I needed to do something, but I wasn't sure what it was. I was tired and sleepy, but I just did not want to go to sleep. I decided to go home, and the drive made me replay everything all over again. It made me see how connected I was to God and Grandma. The feeling I had yesterday was for a reason. I realized that my Tuesdays would never be the same again.

The days are so blurry to me. I remembered Wednesday going home and riding with my sister to get my nephew Dontez from school. He wanted to go (it's always one male in each generation who works through the deaths, funerals, etc.) to school and she allowed him. I remember my sister Chris saying, "I had a feeling that something was wrong. I knew something was wrong but wasn't sure. It was when I got off the phone with you and the back door opened and Mike had left. I was scared because it was dark, and I didn't know how the door opened. That was **Grandma** saying goodbye."

I shook my head in disbelief: "**Grandma** is dead." I thought if I said it enough, my head would understand what my heart was feeling. I could comprehend it all. Still, nope, it had not settled in yet.

The remainder of the time is blurry. I know that I didn't stay for long. I realized that I just did not want to be there. You see, **Grandma** always took care of us during this time. She protected us from people. If we were taking death hard, she made us disappear, and when asked she would say, "Just leave her alone." Everyone respected it, no one went against it because she was **Grandma**. So now who was going to shield me from this? Everyone was in pain in their own way. Grandma was in pain too, but she never showed her pain until the end. Once she realized that everyone was able to get back into their routine, weeks later she would have her cry. So who would be the one to have their cry at the end so that we could have our cries now?

I'm not that strong yet. I'm not that mature in my feelings yet. I'm just not that one yet. I did not want to face the pain, although I felt the pain. Still, returning home I would see that she wasn't there, not just feel it?

So I called Mrs. Linda. She said, "Dear heart, how are you?" Her voice was soft and gentle. I told her I did not want to go home or to the funeral. I refused to go. Mrs. Linda said, "LaQuisha Martin, I need for you to meet me so we can talk." I agreed and she said to me, "Dear, this is your mother's mother. She is hurting too, if not more. You want to be there because if you don't, you will regret it."

"Mrs. Linda, I know she is my mother's mother, but she raised us. My grandma raised us (my sisters and cousins), she was a mother to us." With tears in my eyes, I said, "I can't see her like that. Mrs. Linda, please don't make me go please."

"LaQuisha, I can't make you go, just like I can't make you stay here. I just know you will never forgive yourself if you don't go."

"I will think about it, but I can't promise it." I knew she felt my pain, as I heard myself cry. I cried more because I could hear the pain in my voice. I could hear the gut, core pain and couldn't stop it. This was one time I couldn't hear Grandma say, "Keisha, stop. Don't cry yourself sick." You see, Grandma got us all through the storm. She had the right words to say. She was able to be there for us all and no one felt left out. Grandma could pick up the pieces and know how to put them together again. Grandma made it all right again. So now, who would step in and take the place of Grandma? Who would fix it for us? Who would keep everyone on the right path? Lord, how are we going to get through this one?

The day of the funeral, I seemed shockingly okay. I was surprised myself. I went to view her body and I did not cry, not one time. Yes, I did fix her up a little to be sure she was presentable. She looked like herself to me. There she was, **Grandma.** For the last time this is her. I walked out, thinking, "**Wow,** I'm okay. I am going to get through this one without crying, no one will have to grab me or hold me tight. I got this. See, **Grandma,** maybe it will be me to hold strong for the rest of them. Well, maybe I got this after all."

As we went and gathered at the house, everyone was getting ready. I was still feeling okay. Well, we got to the auditorium, we were lining up and I heard something in my right ear. It was Nikki, she was sick. I went over to her and she said, "Go ahead, I'm okay." I refused, but she insisted, and my cousin Jermaine decided to stay with her (they later made it in).

Well as I was walking in, I heard my name called, "Quisha." As I looked to my left, it was my best friend for life. No matter how long it had been since I had seen her, we were always there for each other. Le'Tasha Hill, my best friend since middle school. Yes sir, she was right there, and I was not surprised. I knew she would be. During the funeral, I was just fine, but then it happened. Someone began a solo. Oh no! It got me every time, and the more I tried to hold it in, the more it hurt my stomach. So, I just let it out. It was a cry like no other. I hated to hear myself cry. As I heard it, I cried harder because I recognized my own pain, and so it hurt more. I wanted to stop. I tried to place my hand over my mouth to prevent myself from crying. I couldn't I just could not do it.

Then it came. It was time to say the final goodbye. As I was crying and walking, the ushers were trying to hold on to me. This part I just hated. "Now look, I'm in my feelings and I know that black people tend to fall smooth out during the viewing of the body. But let me have my moment with my **Grandma** without being held or told not to touch her. **Don't you tell me not to touch my Grandma!**"

I kissed her and she was so cold. I rubbed her face. Still her cheek was cold. I touched her hand and it too was cold. Then my head dropped so low toward the floor as if I had been defeated for **life**. "**Grandma** is dead, and in this moment I cannot change it. I cannot bring her back, I don't understand what happened. When I just saw her a week ago, she was fine, but she was not the same." All of these thoughts came as I looked at her for the last time. I remember moving and running out, trying to get to the car with my head down. I felt like if my head was down, they wouldn't worry about me, just themselves because they lost her too. I felt that if I had my head down, they couldn't say, "OMG, we need to go take care of Keisha." I figured if I held my head down no one would feel the need to rescue me, because in that moment we all needed rescuing.

I remember picking up her obituary and moving really fast to my car. Then I heard my name. It was my girl, yes, Le'Tasha. She hugged me and I broke down, I couldn't hold it any longer. Then I heard another voice, "Keisha, baby, Keisha, baby." Yes, it was my Aunt Janie. She had always been there right by our sides. While Mom was tending to herself and siblings, Aunt Janie had me. They worked well together like that. You would have thought they were sisters separated from birth.

As we all left to head to the burial site, I realized that this was it. This was ending and life went on because time stopped for no one. I remember staring at the casket and feeling like all my hopes, dreams, secrets, laughter, pain, anger, walks, accomplishments, failures were all going down six feet under with her.

"What are we going to do? How are we going to make it? When will the pain stop? Where will we find refuge? Who will be the one to take over and get us through this?"

Through it all, I realized that I never said, "**Why** her, Lord?" I think for me, for as many deaths that our family had experienced, I realized that **Why** was not a question I needed to ask. I didn't want to ask **Him, "Why?"** I wanted the pain to stop. I wanted this to be over. I wanted to feel whole again. I didn't want her back on earth -- that part I knew. Still, how could she be with me, and the pain go away, and she still be in Heaven? I knew that was not possible, but I knew there would come a time when I was not hurting as much.

I realized that **His** plan is never wrong. **His** plan is what allows us to strengthen our **trust** in **Him**. His plan is walking by faith and not by sight. It helped me through some bad days. Still, as I knew that the Lord loved me more than I loved myself, I was human. My pain was still there.

I journaled for a while at work. In the beginning it was every day, then slowly those Tuesdays were not tears, they were laughter. Slowly, I could write to **Grandma** those good times and not dwell on the pain. However, there were other times when in the moment those tears returned, because the grieving process was not done. It still is not.

What I realized was that the first year after her death, I was numb. I could go to her gravesite but could not go to the house. I recall the first time I did since the funeral.

I had just left her gravesite, Xavier and I. I headed down to the house and as I turned that curve, it was a straight shot to her house. I realized that something was not right. I got out of the car and went into the house. Everyone was there except my mother and Aunt Bill (she was the one who was there when my grandma died). I remember laughing for a moment. My cousin Pearl fixed my plate. I bit the hotdog and as I was biting it, I began to look around slowly. My sister Chris was sitting on a sofa, then my baby sister Nikki was sitting on the other sofa (the same sofa my grandma would sit on) as I looked at the corner of the chair that **Grandma** would be. My stomach began to turn, then I looked up and saw her picture. This was when it hit me: "**Grandma** is not here." I gave the plate back to my cousin and asked if she could wrap it up for me. I tried to get out as fast as I could without anyone seeing me cry.

It was too late. My sisters knew it was hitting me hard before I started crying. It was all over my face. So as I ran up the hill, my Aunt Vanice called my name and I could not answer. They all knew why I ran. They all knew it was the first time for me since her funeral. I went and got in the car. My cousin Jerry tried to console me as he tried to fight back tears. My sister Nikki is so strong emotionally you will never see her cry. She came and tried to console me, but I needed to leave. I went to her gravesite and realized that I had just left it thirty minutes ago. I cried out of anger and pain. I called her name many times, I told her I needed her.

To my surprise, the wind blew, and the more I called her name, the more the wind blew. As I sat in the car by her gravesite, I heard her say in my left ear, soft and slow as only she could say it, "Keisha, stop, you are going to make yourself sick." This was what she would always say to me as I cried uncontrollably. I heard her voice. It did not scare me. It calmed me for a moment. In that moment, I realized that if ever I needed her I could call on her and she would answer some way, somehow. Well, the tears started back and the wind started too. It was her way of telling me to get it all out, but don't make myself sick. Finally, I was able to stop crying, and out of the rearview mirror I saw my mother.

She walked up and went over to **Grandma**'s grave. She moved something off and she came back to the car. I **prayed** the entire time, "Lord, please don't let her say anything not right now, Lord, please." Well, the **Lord, Grandma**, and **Mama** were all on the same page with me that day because my mama did not say one word. She walked back to my car and leaned on it with her back to me. We were in silence for a few minutes.

She then said, "You ready to go?"

> *"Hear my prayer, Lord; let my cry for help come to you. Do not hide your face from me when I am in distress. Turn your ear to me; when I call answer me quickly."* Psalm 102:1-2

> *"Honor her for all that her hands have done and let her works bring her praise at the city gate."* Proverbs 31:31

"She is clothed with strength and dignity, she can laugh at the days to come." Proverbs 31:25

"Who could ever find a wife like this one she is a woman of strength in mighty valor! She's full of wealth and wisdom, the price paid for her was greater than many jewels. Her husband has entrusted his heart to her, for she brings him the rich spoils of victory. All throughout her life she brings him what is good, and not evil." Proverbs 31:10-12

"Her children raise up and call her blessed, her husband also and he praises her: many women have done excellently but you surpassed them all." Proverbs 31:28-31 ESV

Chapter Five

SOW IN THE SPIRIT

"Whoever sows to please their flesh, from the flesh will reap destruction; whoever sows to please the Spirit, from the Spirit will reap eternal life. Let us not become weary in doing good, for at the proper time we will reap a harvest if we do not give up" Galatians 6:8-9

My Grandma Virginia was my dad's mother. Grandma had many grandchildren, but she knew them by names and faces. We all had a different relationship with Grandma. My time with her was mostly when I was younger. Grandma Catherine and I went to see Grandma Virginia most times on Saturdays and a lot during the summer months. My days with them together and separate were priceless. Grandma Virginia's voice was to me very distinguished and unique. It's hard to describe, but if you ever heard her you knew how beautiful and unique it was. I loved to listen to her talk because of her voice, but she spoke with such wisdom and God-filled words.

The moments we had on the rocking chairs were priceless. It started with us three musketeers: Catherine, Virginia, and me. Grandma Catherine said, "Come on, Keisha, let's go see Ginia." We walked to Grandma's house. She was always tickled to see us. Grandma Catherine had a stick in her hand. Not a short one, something she could smack a person or thing a mile away with.

Grandma would say, "Catherine where you going with that tree in your hand?" She laughed so hard she held on to her stomach as a few laughing tears came from her eyes.

Grandma Catherine said, "Ginia, I'm ready for anything, come on outside and talk."

As we sat on the porch, I sat on the bottom of the porch and my grandmas were in the rocking chairs. They made the loudest noises, but once you got used to them, brought on totally different meaning.

I remembered after my two uncles passed, Uncle John and David, my Grandma Catherine went down to visit with Grandma. Grandma Virginia started to share how she felt and how things happened and then she got quiet. Usually kids were not allowed to be in grown folk conversations, but they both told me, "You can stay out here, but you don't repeat what you hear." So I won't repeat it not even now.

I turned around, not sure why she stopped. All I heard was the rocking chairs and both of my grandmas looked straight ahead at the road. I realized they both had lost under their Spiritual Resume. Grandma Virginia had buried two of her sons and Grandma Catherine had buried five of her sons. I didn't know how they felt (and still don't want to know) to bury children. I could see their pain, but as they rocked I saw **strength, faith, wisdom, wounded warriors**. As the rocking chairs continued to squeak, their minds wandered. Never did I ask what they were thinking, because if they wanted to share, they never would've stopped talking. I was young, but being around those two I obtained a lot of wisdom.

During those talks on the porch, Grandma Virginia said, "Keisha baby, don't go behind those bushes with those boys."

Grandma Catherine said, "Ain't nothing in bushes but rats and thieves."

I was young, elementary, maybe beginning of middle school, but I had no idea what they spoke about. Still, I never went behind any bushes with a little boy, big boy, white boy, black boy, no boy at all. I listened very well. Once I kept on living, I understood what they meant and was glad I listened. LOL. I recall many of my moments with Grandma Virginia, and the ones I do have impacted me greatly.

Grandma Virginia had a phone in her living room, and it was the type of phone where you put your finger into the holes and turned it. LOL. She didn't have an answering machine. Grandma was usually in the kitchen or her bedroom, even if she was on the sofa in the living room. You had to give her time to get to the phone. Lord, that phone rang and rang. If you wanted to strengthen your patience, all you had to do was call Grandma. Grandma had no sense of urgency about getting to the phone. I guess she figured if it was important enough, they would wait. If not, they would call back or not. LOL. She took her time, but she always answered.

Remind you of anyone? God is an Almighty God. His timing is better than our own, but when He answers it is always on time. Or is that just me and mine?

Well, I had my driver's license and I wanted a car. I spoke to my Grandma and asked if Grandpa John L would help me find one. Well, he did, and I was so excited. It was a burgundy Cadillac. Man, I loved that car, but it didn't last long. Something happened to the motor. I went to the house with my voice shaking because I wanted to cry, but didn't. I asked Grandma if she would ask Grandpa to help me. Well, he came through the door and looked through the mail. I told him what was wrong with the car, but he didn't seem to pay me much attention. Grandma got up from the sofa and followed him in the kitchen. I'm not sure what was said, but he came out and said he would have someone to look at it or just give me my money back. Well, long story short, I got my money back, but I wanted the car.

Grandma said, "Baby, God makes no mistakes. That just wasn't your car." I didn't understand at that time, but Grandma Virginia always spoke with the Spirit.

While in college I had enough money to get my own car and made payments. I drove home and showed Grandma. She opened the door and said, "Keisha baby, I didn't know that was you."

I said, "Grandma, I bought a car. It took a year, but I got one."

Grandma said, "See, baby, what God has for you no man can keep you from it. Prayer changes things."

What gave me pause was that I never prayed for a car. Just because I wasn't didn't mean Grandma wasn't.

Well, it didn't stop there. When I was pregnant with Xavier, I went to see both grandmas to help me figure out how to have this baby. Xavier was overdue and so was my body, soul, mind and spirit. Grandma Catherine didn't help, so I headed to Grandma Virginia's. I knocked on the door and as she looked out, I saw her smile.

"Baby, what you doing out and about?"

"Grandma, I'm tired. Is there something I can do to get him to come?"

Grandma said, "Keisha, God has something amazing right here (as she touched my stomach). There's a reason why he ain't come yet."

"But Grandma." I started to cry, I was so exhausted, couldn't sleep or eat, emotional.

My head lowered and Grandma said, "Oh, hear baby, women been giving birth since the beginning of time. Don't rush him here." It was soothing as she rocked me while she had her arms wrapped around me.

Well, a few days later, Grandma Virginia called Grandma Catherine and asked "Catherine, have you heard from Keisha? She's in my spirit."

Grandma Catherine said, "She's in your spirit and I have her labor pains. That child is in labor, Ginia."

Grandma Catherine and Virginia later told me the story. It seemed whenever Grandma Catherine had a pain, Grandma Ginia said, "Lord help 'em both." We all laughed so hard.

As I got older, my visits with my Grandma Virginia declined. That was my fault. It had nothing to do with her. She knew the reason, but still I should have done better. I went a few times to see her as her health declined. I didn't want to see her that way, but I did. I never cried while I was there. I would leave, head to Charlotte, and cried in the car. It brought so many memories of how she was so strong, but in that moment her body was weak. It was hard to see her or even imagine her that way. So all I could do was pray. I knew to pray because she did it for me.

It reminded me of a time I was truly heartbroken. I drove from Charlotte and went to see Grandma Virginia. Lord, I knew Grandma Catherine had already told her the news. As I walked in, she said, "Hey, Keisha baby, come on in. Keisha, you look defeated."

I couldn't respond verbally, I just cried. My grandma walked me over to the sofa. Her Bible was on the sofa, so I could tell she was reading before I came. Grandma told me to sit down and I did.

Grandma said, "Baby, I know you're hurting and I know what that pain feels like, but I need you to give it to God."

As I listened, I realized I didn't know how to give it to God. I was so angry at God.

Grandma Virginia said, "I need for you to start reading your Bible. Write down how you feel because you write those poems all the time, and now start writing to God. God can handle you being angry. **He** knows your pain."

I listened and cried. Then it got quiet. I was exhausted from crying. My head ended up on Grandma's lap. I opened my eyes. Apparently, I had drifted off to sleep. I raised up and Grandma was reading her Bible. You know, I believe she prayed over me. My pain was still there, but I got some rest. I wasn't sure how I was going to get through it, but I knew I had a praying grandmother. So as I drove back to Charlotte with that memory, I realized that I made it through that storm because my grandmother never stopped praying for me.

This last memory, I am not sure if I can make it through it, but I have a praying grandmother so I will be fine. Grandma Virginia's health had truly declined. I went to get her a gift for Christmas. I always bought her bedroom shoes, just like a grandchild. This time I decided on a couple of nightgowns. As I looked, what I thought would take ten to fifteen minutes took an hour.

The salesperson said, "I see you are putting a lot into this."

It wasn't about the nightgown, it was the nervousness I felt. I was so anxious and I didn't know why. She helped me decide to get them both and a robe. As I went to my uncle's house, I felt like I was out of place. My Uncle Dan was in the yard and Jeanette was in the house. I took the gifts into Grandma's room, but I didn't look at her. I walked out of the room and sat in the living room for a while. Uncle Dan kept walking back and forth in her room. I knew he knew, and this was why I felt uneasy. Something was about to happen. I finally went back in and I went up to her bed.

I said, "Grandma, it's me, Keisha. Grandma, open your eyes, please open your eyes. Grandma, I'm getting married. His name is Dennis. Can you open your eyes?"

I started to silently cry as my head dropped hard and hit my hand as it was resting on her bedrail. It brought back the memory of the moment I cried on her lap. You see, Grandma said before I left, "Keisha baby, God will work everything out for your good. You will find joy again."

So I raised my head back up and I whispered, "Grandma, it's me Keisha, please open your eyes." Tears fell from my eyes and I felt like if she did, I would be okay. Well, as I looked back up and said, "Grandma, I love you, but I will let you rest," she opened her eyes. She wasn't looking at me, but she opened her eyes and then she closed them.

For me, that was her saying, "I hear you."

For me, that was her saying, "God worked it out for your good."

For me that was her saying, "Now it's you who have to pray for others. You are now that **Wounded Warrior Newly Nourished Making Movements.**"

I kissed her on her forehead and said, "I love you, now rest." I left there and knew that was her goodbye to me.

A week and a half or more later, I got a call from Jeannette and I knew what it was. I needed for her to tell me. I needed for her to say the words so my heart could register what my ears heard.

Jeanette asked, "Where is Xavier?"

I said, "In his room, just tell me. I am stronger now."

You see, reader, I had just been through a spiritual storm with my cousin Pearl. If you have not read Pearlie Gates, please do so. This journey with Pearl allowed me to free myself from the fear of death. God strengthened me in a way that I never knew I could be strengthened.

So she said, "Keisha, your grandma passed today." She paused, waiting to see just how I would respond.

I said, "Thank you for telling me, I got to go now."

Jeannette wanted to be sure I was okay and I told her I was. After getting off the phone, I cried in the bathroom. I needed my moment to take it all in. Although I knew it was coming, still it didn't settle in until I heard the words. I told Dennis, who was in the bedroom. He did what he knew to do, which was hug me. We went into Xavier's room and I told him. It wasn't until I saw Xavier that my tears flowed heavily, my cry was heavier. I heard my cry and cried harder. Dennis stepped out of the room into the hallway. The cry for him was painful. He couldn't change the outcome. He could not take the pain away and I knew he felt helpless. I felt helpless. So I went into the bathroom. Xavier and Dennis spoke.

I got in the bed and I said, "D, I need for you to watch Xavier."

Dennis replied, "Xavier told me to watch after you, so that is what I will do."

I said, "No, if Xavier is okay, I will be okay."

Dennis said, "Xavier said if you were okay, he would be okay."

In that moment, he realized the bond Xavier and I had. I went to the funeral. Dennis wasn't able to attend. Xavier was there, and before we went in, I said, "Xavier, we will sit in the back. I don't want to see her in the casket. Are you going to be okay?"

He said, "As long as you are good, Mom, I'm good."

Well, I went to sit down in the back row, but the ushers escorted Xavier to the front. I couldn't let him sit there without me. He looked back at me to let me know he was okay, but I went to be with him. I had my head downward. I didn't want to see her in the casket. I just didn't want to cry. I looked over at my Uncle Dan. He looked lost, helpless, and I couldn't take that pain away. I dropped my head and continued to look at my shoes. I did okay until the solo. I don't know why, but a song brought those tears out that I wanted to hold back. I tried not to cry loudly. I tried to keep my head down and shed my tears in silence. It hurt my stomach so bad, but I did it. I didn't get close to the gravesite. I didn't want that memory in my head, but I have it.

My Grandma Virginia was a woman with much character, wisdom, faith, and a pillar of strength. She had been through some things, but she stood in it strong and victorious. It reminded me of scripture:

"She opens her mouth with wisdom, and the teaching of kindness is on her tongue." Proverbs 31:26

> *"Peace I leave with you; my peace I give you.*
> *I do not give to you as the world gives. Do*
> *not let your hearts be troubled and do not be*
> *afraid". John 14:27*

Chapter Six

WHY NOT ME?

Psalm 91

He who dwells in the shelter of the most high will rest in the shadow of the almighty. I will say to the Lord, "My refuge and my fortress, my God, in whom I trust." Surely he will save me from the fowler's snare and from the deadly pestilence. He will cover me with his feathers, and under his wings I will find refuge; His faithfulness will be my shield and rapture. I will not fear the terror of night, nor the arrow that flies by day, nor the pestilence that stocks in the darkness, nor the plague that destroys at midday. A thousand may fall at my side, ten thousand at my right hand, but it will not come near me.

I will only observe with my eyes and see the punishment of the wicked. If I make the most high my dwelling-even

the Lord who is my refuge-- then no harm will be before me, no disaster will come near my tent. For he will command his angels to take charge over me to guard me in all my ways; They will lift me up in their hands so that I will not strike my foot against the stone. I will tread upon the lion and the cobra; I will trample the great lion and the serpent.

"because she loves me, says the LORD, "I will rescue LaQuisha; I will protect her, for she acknowledges my name.

LaQuisha will call upon me, and I will answer her; I will be with her in trouble, I will deliver her and honor her. With long life I will satisfy her and show her my salvation"...

I must shed some light on someone special. She had been struggling for some time. She had her own share of loss, pain, heartaches, and heartbreaks. God counted each and every one of her tears and recorded them for His deliverance of this bondage she was in. She knew what she had to do, but she kept trying to do it in her own strength. Each time we spoke, our conversation began to change. We began to speak more about God than the situations we were in. We began to praise God for what we could not see but we knew would come to pass. I told my sister Nikki, "God has something amazing for you. Just keep on moving forward." I knew she was tired, but I knew what God had spoken.

So, I wanted to take it away from her. God said, "No ma'am, that is not your task. Stay on My roadmap, LaQuisha."

"Lord, my sister is hurting. Lord, help her."

God said, "I see all her pain and tears. She is in the position I need her to be in. I hear what you can't, I see what you don't, I know her heart."

My sister was tired, but she kept moving forward. She felt she was moving in quicksand, but she took one step at a time. One morning, I woke up with a song on my heart, "I told the storm." I sent the text out to family. Nikki and Jeannette were in my spirit. As I sat on my praying porch, I began to pray. Later that day, my sister texted to say, "they have a home." You see, they were thinking small about their house, but they were moving forward. Each time they tried, something blocked them.

What they soon heard was how God said, "You are faithful and I have seen your tears. Today, I bless you with what I designed especially for you and your family. A **home,** not just a house. You see, I needed you in this position to advance you into My will. Had you walked away, you would have missed your blessing."

My sister said, "Keisha, do you remember our conversation? How I told you that the trials and tribulation you went through were to make you stronger so, **Why not you, Why not me?**"

Now looking over my life, all the things I went through, I questioned God: "Why me? Lord, why did I have to lose the desire to play basketball? The one thing that gave me joy. Lord, why did I lose my loved ones, the most important men in my life? Lord, my motherhood journey, I had so many mistakes and uncomfortable moments. Lord, **why me**? Lord, my grandmothers were the persons who gave me the meaning of what life was. They shaped me into the woman I am today. I'm in a world without them. **Why me?**"

As I looked back, I saw the growth with the trials, tribulations, and storms Nikki spoke about.

So now I say, "God, **Why Not Me**? I'm a Wounded Warrior Newly Nourished Making Meaningful Movements, why not me? I've seen my share of struggles, pain, death, heartaches. God, why not me? I've prayed through some things, cried, disappointments after disappointments. Why not me? I see, Lord, You are a jealous God. No one or nothing should be before You. This happened to prepare me, to strengthen me, to build my relationship with You, and to develop my Spiritual Resume."

So now, I have something to look back on for the next ... whatever that next is. I can and will say, "He helped me through my past, He will help me through my present and future." I'm building a resume one trial, one tribulation, one storm at a time. It's giving me testimonial experiences to share with others. It's strengthening me in ways I never imagined. I will have delays, but not setbacks. I will have moments of weakness, but God, Your strength will guide me through. I may have times of sorrow and despair, but joy will come in the morning. Yes Lord, I see **Why It's Me!**

As I continue with this journey I call life, I will continue to build my Spiritual Resume. I will continue to move forward, knowing that I have something I must accomplish. I have something that I desire more than basketball, loved ones gone and present, more than homes and cars. My final task is to be at Your feet, Father, to wash Your feet with my hair and perfume. For when I stand before You, Father, I pray You say, "Well done and welcome home."

So I come to you, my readers. What will you do to allow your Spiritual Resume to grow? Will you place God in a box and live life in fear and out of the eyes of those who are trying Him? Will you feel less than a conqueror and sit in what you wish you should have done, could have done, or thought about? Will you continue to try the same thing over and over again, feeling like you can do it without Him? Grandma Catherine said, "How is that working out for you? Have you finished ramming your head into that wall yet?" Grandma Virginia said, "What is for you there will be no man to stand in God's way. Keep on praying, write it down, and talk to God."

You see, He sent some strong Wounded Warriors who were Newly Nourished and Made Meaningful Movements in my life. Time and time again, my grandmothers and mother brought me back to my Father. They prayed for me, they prayed over me, they nurtured my pain, they talked to God about me, and they showed me how to talk to Him for myself. Mama Bernice said, "Go into your closet, baby, and give it to God."

Now, I'm the Wounded Warrior Newly Nourished Making Meaningful Movements in your life. Now I am telling you to "Try Him, seek His face, His word, His presence and see how you are renewed, restored, replenished, rejuvenated, rewarded, reminded, redeemed, revised and then **watch** Him return."

ACKNOWLEDGMENTS

My husband Dennis, this book came to life because of you and the ride from Atlanta. Here's to being **quiet!** Thank you and I Love you.

Xavier, baby, I am always thankful to God for you. You are joy. Son, the love I have for you is unconditional and never failing. Thank you for all your support and encouragement. Love you.

To my mother Bernice, thank you for all your support and love. "Go into your closet, baby, and give it to God." Mama, I went in and came out with my Spiritual Resume. Love you.

My sister Chris I thank you for all your love, support, and understanding. Love you

My sister Nikki, girl we have come a long way and we are moving forward. Thank you for allowing me to be apart of this journey with you. I love you.

Jeannette, I have to say once more you are the big sister I needed. You have been there for me from the beginning of time. I love you so much. Thank you for all that you do for our family and me. Love you.

To the Martin and Green Family, I thank you all for all your love and support. I thank you for the laughter and the genuine care we provide for each other. Love you.

Mrs. Linda and Mr. Cedric "Pops," I thank you once again for who you are in my life. This was the beginning of our journey and I'm so grateful for your obedience to God. I'm learning so much from you and Pops. Thank you. Love you both.

Shay and Joann, I do thank you both for being in these moments with me. Time and time again, your support was different but touched me the same. You are more than friends, you are my sisters. Thank you both for just being. Love you.

LeTasha, I want to thank you for then and now. No matter the distance or the time in between. You have and will be "my sister." Love you.

Johnathan, God has truly used in my life. Thank you for your prayers and encouragement. Love you my brother

Stan, my dear brother, thank you for this opportunity for your guidance and steadfast efforts. Love you my brother

To my extended family, thank you for the laughs, cries, support, time spent, and advice. Love you all.

To the loved ones gone, I say thank you for then and now. I had to go through some things to get to this point in my life. Yes, it was hard, yes it hurt sometimes, but God. We miss you, and for me, I would not wish you back on earth because each one of you deserve to be with our Heavenly Father.

THANK YOU, FATHER

Father, just when I want to throw in the towel, I hear Your voice and I soak my heart in Your words. I pray they remain on my tongue and embedded in my heart. Lord, my Father, You want me to go higher, filled with new experiences, enhance my knowledge/ income, surround me with new people, and visit new places. The only way I can do all these things, I have to stay connected to YOU, your word, and to refuse to settle. I hear You, Lord, when You say:

"For God has not given us a spirit of fear, but of power and of love and of a sound mind." 2 Timothy 1:7

"And my God shall supply all your needs according to His riches in glory by Christ Jesus." Philippians 4:19

"Now thanks be to God who always leads us in triumph in Christ, and through us diffuses the fragrance of His knowledge in every place." 2 Corinthians 2:14

CPSIA information can be obtained
at www.ICGtesting.com
Printed in the USA
LVHW080819071221
705493LV00007B/149